Will You Obey the Word of God?

A Praise and Worship Syllabus

Will You Obey the Word of God?

A Praise and Worship Syllabus

BY: Pastor Eleanor A. Murray
of
The New Light Ministries in Amarillo, Texas

© Copyright 2012 Eleanor A. Murray

All rights reserved. This book is protected under the copyright laws of the United States of America. No portion of this book may be reproduced in any form, without the written permission of the publisher. Permission granted on request.

Unlock Publishing House
231 West Hampton Place
Capitol Heights, MD 20743
www.unlockpublishinghouse.com
1 (240) 619-3852

Edited by Mary Arnold

Cover design by Wallicia McCaskill

Unlock Publishing House is not responsible for any content or determination of work. All information is solely considered as the point of view of the author.

ISBN: 978-0-9855261-7-7

Dedication

I dedicate this book to my husband, Bishop Richard Murray, and my two anointed daughters, Teresa Murray and Kimberly Murray Houston, for their constant encouragement. They inspire me with confidence to continue teaching Praise and Worship.

My husband always says, "Mama knows how to cook-up and serve a good meal" – meaning when Mama teaches the word of God, imparting it through instruction, the spiritual man will be completely nourished.

My to anointed daughters use a slang word whenever they describe my method of teaching of Praise and Worship. They say, "Mama is a 'Beast' in teaching Praise and Worship" – meaning Mama is extremely successful when conveying the message of genuine Praise and Worship and there are not too many people able to compare with her teaching and demonstration. Many people have said that God has given me a method that produces many offspring in Praise and Worship; and that God has given me a special technique to teach people how to invoke the presence of God into their situations.

Acknowledgments

I would like to thank my publisher, Pastor Dawn Harvey, and editor, Mary Arnold, for the time and energy spent focusing on the presentation of this book; making sure it represents God in an excellent way.

This book is a result of years of leading Praise and Worship and invoking the presence of God into worship services.

I give thanks to Donna Louise and Kathy Shetterly for helping with the foundation of this syllabus, and for their unselfish love to layout the outline that helped me get started.

Many thanks to New Light Ministries of Amarillo, Texas, Felicia Cotton, Diane Mclaughlin, Wayne and Wanda Nelson, Elaine Loftis, Ethel Boney Williams and Jean Campbell for organizing, decorating and setting up the tabernacle and for the photographs provided to submit for publishing purposes.

Also, thanks to the prisoners of the Neal Unit in Amarillo, Texas for building the Tabernacle and basically donating it to the New Light Ministries.

I would like to thank Prophetess Gloria Archie of Houston, Texas for her enduring prayers and prophetic word that have supported me throughout the ministry that God has called for me.

I thank all of my friends and family for their moral and spiritual support, their sacrifices of time and attention which have afforded this period of affirmation during the creative process of this syllabus.

Table of Contents

Introduction 11

Worship 15

Spirit 25

Cornerstones 27

Proclaiming the Virtues 33

Embraced in His Love – Enveloped in
His Glory and Endued with His Power 39

Instructions for Offering Praise and Worship 51

Command Them to Praise,
They are Subject to the Holy Spirit in You 59

Demonstration and Procedures When
We Enter into the Holy of Holies 63

Suggested Hebrew Words of Praise 77

Holy of Holies 83

Test Questions 91

Answers to Test Questions 95

Now We are Embraced in His Love – Enveloped
in His Glory and Endued with His Power 97

Photographs of Interest 119

Introduction

As we experience life, we must come to realize that our strength comes from God. As we seek Him through prayer, praise and worship, we will begin to understand the true joy of being in the Presence of God. As the aroma of our praise and worship surrounds God's Throne, He will allow His Glory/Presence to fill our situation and circumstances here on earth.

> *2 Timothy 3:16 (KJV)*
>
> *[16]All scripture is given by inspiration of God, and is profitable for doctrine, for reproof, for correction, for instruction in righteousness:*

The entire Bible was given to us by the very idea of God. God expressed the revelation of His will and mind by literally breathing the Word of God into existence so that we might be taught, rebuked, improved and trained in how we should live. Through the instruction of God's word, He prepares us and fully equips us to be the Praise and Worshippers that will glorify His name; and teach us the position or posture of true worship while we are surrounded by His Glory. God's word is the coach that will guide us toward triumph praise and worship while entering into and actually being in His presence.

> *Romans 8:5-8 KJV*
>
> *[5]For they that are after the flesh do mind the things of the flesh; but they that are after the Spirit the things of the Spirit.*
>
> *[6]For to be carnally minded is death; but to be spiritually minded is life and peace.*

7Because the carnal mind is enmity against God: for it is not subject to the law of God, neither indeed can be.

8So then they that are in the flesh cannot please God

We must understand that the flesh will not be able to boast in the presence of God and surely cannot be justified in His sight (I Corinthians 1:29 and Romans 3:20); we must humble ourselves before our majesty as we enter into His prescnce.

Humans are made in the image of God and are triune beings made of a spirit, soul and body. The soul combined with the body makes up our flesh. Like this, the *Flesh* is the natural part of us and not the born again spiritual man that has been quickened alive. The *Soul* is our will, emotions, personality or intellect. The *Body* has strong desires, cravings and an appetite which will lust for the things of the world. It is quite clear that this part of us cannot receive the entire honor in God's presence.

People who live their lives according to the flesh usually have their attitudes fashioned by the thing of the flesh, but those who live according to the Spirit of God have their view on the things of God. The flesh is an enmity against God and indeed is not subject to the laws of God, therefore cannot please God. One must not respond to the leadings of the flesh but more to the Word of God for direction. The flesh is the old nature and that part of us detests being in the presence God. The flesh desires to be exalted and when in the presence of God, it is not able to be superior (Romans 6: 11 and 8:7-9), therefore it is hostile and in opposition when in His Presence.

The flesh demands to be on exhibit and will intellectually have one think that it is ignorant or emotional to praise God in the way He instructs. A good example of the flesh's response to Clamors of Praise is:

- It does not take all of that –
- The praise is too loud,
- The clapping is really not necessary...
- One should keep silent in God's Presence

But we are instructed in the word of God in Psalms 41:1 "O clap your hands, all ye people and shout to God with the voice of triumph," and Psalms 33:3 says "Sing unto him a new song; play skillfully with a loud noise," therefore, we must obey.

The authoritative Word of God will instruct us in the way God desires us to praise and worship Him. It will instruct, teach and guide us in the way which we should go; however, we are not to be like an unintelligent horse or mule which will not obey unless they are controlled by a bridle and bit (Psalms 32:8 NET). We are not to be as the mule that is stubborn and will not comply with God's instructions. God has laid the blue print to follow and obey in order for us to be thorough in praise and worship. God's people should not have to be pumped, pushed, reminded or begged to obey His instructions. God's people should not have to be supervised and directed when in praise and worship; because we should "**Be**" praise and worshippers and not "Just **Do**" worship as puppets. When one becomes a true worshipper, praise and worship will flow from the heart and they automatically enter into God's presence with thanksgiving and into His courts with praise. At the same time, they are expressing their thanks unto Him vocally and blessing His name simply because He is God and His mercy endures forever. The very existence of God's people should be Praise and Worship, not just for a performance or an act, but a lifestyle.

Worship

Worship is associated with attributing honor, reverence or worth to God just because He is God. Worship is the occupation of the soul toward God Himself. As we offer worship to the Divine God, it is adoration in word, gesture, prayer, confession and songs of praise and thanksgiving; that extols God the Father and Jesus the Son. **Songs of Praise** should contain ministry about our God as well as toward God; but **Songs of Worship** should be directly to God unswervingly and only God; so that He will be blessed and reverenced and no other.

In the New Testament Church, worship is that of joy and thanksgiving in the face of God's gracious redemption of mankind in Jesus Christ. We worship for the past, present and future in combination; because God was, is and is to come in present with His people in worship. For as Jesus expressed through His Apostle John to the seven churches in the Book of Revelation, He said: "...Grace be unto you, and peace, from him which is, and which was, and which is to come; and from the seven Spirits which are before his throne." Therefore, we should praise and worship God for what He has done, is doing and will do for us in the future.

In St. John 4:20-24, Jesus describes and makes clear the definition of worship to the Samaritan woman at Jacob's well. The Samaritan woman mentioned a place of worship in comparison to the Jews worshipping at Jerusalem and Jesus' told her that the location had nothing to do with genuine worship. The worship that God seeks is the worship that is in Spirit and in Truth from the heart. Religious worship usually puts God's people in a box and their worship becomes ritualistic and traditional rather than after the rudiment of Christ. When the location or a church building becomes more important than just invoking the presence of God, this worship can become hypercritical and eventually role play. Our entire aim and whole focus should be targeted to Jesus, because He should be the only recipient of Worship. Our intentions, plans, and endeavor in Worship should be Jesus only. We should enter into praise and worship with our sights set on Jesus, aspiring to have an encounter with Him and offering our sacrifice of praise to God by proclaiming the glory of Jesus' name and giving Him continual thanks.

Only when the spirit of a man communes with God, does true worship take place. When we commune with God, we converse and feel at one with Him as in a relationship. We connect and communicate with Him, conveying words of love as we fellowship with Him. When we are worshipping, we should focus and listen carefully for our master to speak to our hearts. We must pay close attention to the move of God and all ears should be open to hear what the Holy Spirit has to say to the church. We must be alert, not slumbering or talking to our neighbor or allowing any other distractions, but tunneling our vision upon the King of Kings and the Lord of Lords, who is God Almighty.

When we address God in Worship, we speak and acknowledge Him for being Lord, King and Majesty. Worship is strictly to God. When we address Him as Lord, we realize He is in authority over us, and everything we are, have and do; whether it be in the past, present or future. When we address Him as King, we have come to the understanding that He is the principle peace in our lives and is number one in importance to us. When we concentrate on Him as Majesty, we have come to realize that He is the reigning influence that rules our entire existence. The Father seeks genuine worshippers who will worship Him in Spirit, and in Truth.

Worship is given to God alone and not to man. True worship is when man, through his spirit, arrives at a place of a relationship and intimacy with God. The spirit man is invisible and immortal and God is invisible and immortal. Proverbs 20:27 says "The spirit of man is the candle of the Lord, searching all the inward parts of the belly." I believe, when we are truly worshipping in Spirit and Truth, our candle is lit and because God seeks such to worship, the brightness and glow of the candle, even in the midst of congregational worship, is ignited and will begin to burn with passion to draw nigh to God. Once we draw nigh to God, He will draw nigh to us and in this process our hands and hearts will be cleansed; and as a result, the intimacy begins.

There are three Greek words for Worship which are:

1. Latreuno – meaning public

2. Sebomia – meaning to Reverence in Awe

3. Proskueno – meaning to Pros (toward) – Kueno (to Kiss); # 4352 Strong's Concordance means to adore, to do reverence, to pay homage to: ...for the Father seeketh (Prosknuneo) such to worship him. Proskunetes ("pros-koo-nay-tace") #4353 Strong's Concordance means worshipper – "...the true worshippers

(proskunetes) shall worship the Father in sprit an in truth (St. John 4:23)

Proskuneo in the English language eventually became worth-ship. The word "worth" has to do with "value." The suffix "ship" denotes a state or condition. Proskuneo is to value our Lord in a state of dignity as we honor His position as Lord. Worship is an art and God looks at us as His art of creation. As we worship, we are placing an importance and merit upon our God that none other deserves.

If we had to compare the particular origin of this word "Proskuneo," we could compare it to words such as courtship, friendship, or fellowship. Proskuneo has an Eastern usage describing kissing the ground in the presence of a potentate or bowing in obedience before a ruler. At one time this word was a word of warm affection describing a puppy kissing the hand of his master or crouching down at the feet of his master. Strong's Concordance relates worship to reverence, holy and hallowed things – to adore; bow to; honor.

Therapeuo (ther-ap-yoo-o) #2323 in Strong's Concordance means to serve, to wait on, to attend, and to do service to deity. In the King James Version, the word for worship means supply; minister or serve. Latreuo ("lat-ryoo'-o") meaning to serve, to be bound to, to minister to the Lord, to render spiritual homage. We are to serve God as if we are waiters or waitresses; not as though God needs our services, but because we reverence Him.

Worship is therapeutic and can be described as a form of therapy; because praise and worship can be beneficial to us even as an instrument of healing. It will uplift and sooth our entire being and is like a treatment to our souls. When we invoke the presence of God into our situation His attributes show up. One of His attributes is healing; He is Jehovah Rapha/Rophe/Yahweh Ropheka the Lord who is the healer. Jesus is the Great Physician and is the one who can heal both body and soul. As we worship, the Sun of Righteousness will rise with healing in his wings for the people who reverence and respect His name and His people will leave His presence healed (Malachi 4:2). Worship can also be the remedy toward rehabilitation to good health because in the presence of the Lord is the fullness of joy and the joy of the Lord is our strength; once joy has been manifested, which is in unison with a merry heart, worship becomes medicine to our bodies, minds and souls (Psalm 16:11; Nehemiah 8:10). Proverbs 17:22 says: "...a merry heart does good like a medicine..." In Exodus 15:26, God said, "If you will diligently obey the Lord your God, and do what is right in his sight, and pay attention to his commandments, and keep all his statutes, then all the diseases that I brought on the Egyptians I will not bring on you, for **I, the Lord, am your healer**."

Joy is an emotion often expressed audibly and is usually a noisy worship; we are to make a joyful and loud noise unto our God with rejoicing, singing and praise. When the word instructs us to be joyful in glory and sing aloud, it is endorsing us to be joyful in God's glory; nevertheless, we can choose to be joyful and sing or reject the offer. (Psalms 98:4; 105:43; 149:5)

Joy in the Hebrew language is *Rinnah* (*Ree-nah*): a shout of rejoicing; shouting loud; cheering in triumph; singing. The word describes the kind of joyful shouting at the time of a great victory. It describes the jubilation of the righteous when the wicked is eliminated and says God danced over His beloved people, with singing or a shout of joy. Joy can be expressed because God's people know the outcome is controlled by the Almighty God. In the lifestyle of **Praise and Worship**, we must come to the realization that the Joy of the Lord is our strength (Neh. 8:10).

Praise is associated with speaking well of God and to Him and others for what He has done, is doing or will do. With exuberance and enthusiasm we thank God and tell others of His goodness and Praise Him for His deeds and actions. A praise gathering is a celebration of God's might, power and purpose. In Psalms 148 we find that the entire creation is commanded to Praise the Lord for He is the Creator and Sovereign King of the world. He has made his people victorious, and given all his loyal followers specific reason to praise. One reason is that we have been redeemed from the curse of the law and the word instructs us in Psalms 107:2: "Let the redeemed of the LORD say so, Whom He has redeemed from the hand of the adversary" (NASB). In other words, if you have been redeemed from the power of the enemy, speak out and tell somebody about the goodness of the Lord. Speak out and tell God how good He is, has been and will be. As we begin to speak out into the atmosphere the praises of God and openly declare His praises, the aroma of our praise and worship will surround God's throne and He will inhabit our praise. God will then allow His Glory, His presence to fill our situation and circumstances here on earth (Psalms 22:3). The Almighty El-Shaddai/El-Shadday, God Almighty the God of Blessings will show up; and when He comes, He brings all of His attributes with him.

With reference to the scripture that God will inhabit our praises, we realize that God never leaves us nor forsakes us, but when we focus on Him, we become more conscious that He is present. When we tunnel our vision and center our attention on the King of Kings, we are mindful of His presence.

When we offer up thanksgiving; pouring out our sacrificial praises to God from our lips, God's presences will abode in our midst manifesting all of His attributes. The Lord our God in the midst of us will prove his self mighty to save. Zephaniah 3:17 makes us aware that the Lord our God who is with us, is a victorious warrior and in the center of our praise and worship; He will rejoice over us with great gladness, calm our fears and sing over us with songs of joy. When His Presence inhabits our praise, His qualities prove Him to be strong on our behalf.

In the midst of our Praise and Worship, He is:

- *Jehovah - Jireh* – *He brings provisions and success*
- *Jehovah – Rophe* – *He brings healing and soundness*
- *Jehovah- Tsidkenu* – *He brings His righteousness from sin*
- *Jehovah – M'kaddesh* – *He brings sanctification from sin*
- *Jehovah – Shalom* – *He brings peace for our Spirit Man*
- *Jehovah – Shammah* – *He is always there to provide the need*
- *Jehovah – Nissi* – *He is our banner, protection and victory*
- *Jehovah – Rohi* – *He is our security*

When we enter into God's spiritual gates with thanksgiving and into His courts with praise; we should enter being thankful unto Him and blessing His name because He is good and His mercy endures forever (Psalms 100:4).

As we enter into the presence of God, the Word of God reminds us that He will never break the covenant that He has made with us nor will He alter the things that have come from His lips (Psalms 89:34). As a result, we enter into His presence with praise and allow our praise to respond to God's revelation of Himself and proclaim His merits and worth. We enter into His presences speaking well of Him with exuberance and thanking Him for His mighty acts. We extend our thanks, showing forth praise to Him with excitement because He has brought us out of darkness and translated us into the Kingdom of His dear Son. We command our very being to extol God's virtues and express gratitude for the victories He has won in our lives.

When we praise and worship, God's presence will reside and occupy the room which we occupy and sit down in our circumstances, being the Almighty El-Shaddai/El-Shadday, the "God of more than enough," the "Almighty God," the "God who nourishes;" for that God will enthrone on our praises, manifesting His qualities and worth.

St. John 4:24 teaches us that "God is spirit, and the people who worship him must worship in Spirit and Truth." The noun for Spirit means to breathe or to blow. It can be described as air set in motion by breathing and blowing out into the atmosphere and also depicted as life itself. When we open our mouths and offer up a praise with the fruit of our lips giving thanks, and speak words of praise and worship into our situation; we release the breath of the New Creation in us.

Psalms 150:6 instructs us to "Let everything that has breath praise the LORD." Praise the LORD!"

In other words, let everything breathing, praise the Lord or everything that continues to exist have been instructed to praise the true and living God. We have a choice to praise the Lord or not to praise Him. We must consent to praise our Lord and forbid not our praise. We must yield our wills to praise and bring our choices under subjection to God, because our fleshly wills chooses not to glorify God. I believe since I Corinthians 1:29 lets us know that no flesh will glory in God's presence, that part of our being would prefer not to be in the presence of God. Our wills or flesh desires to be exalted and glorified and anyone that desires glory, must only glory in the Lord and not self. The power to choose has been given to us by God, by which we must decide to obey the Word of God and praise Him as instructed. Therefore, we must let our breath go forth in praise thereby preferring praise and worship to God rather than self or man.

Upon that breath of Praise and Worship, the God of our Salvation will enthrone and when He enthrones, He will bring all of His attributes along with Him. As an example, if we were to blow into our hand, we can feel an air of breath. Second, if we blow our breath upon a mirror, we can see a reflection of fog, vapor, mist or haze upon that mirror; these examples let us know that when we breathe, an air, vapor, fog or mist is set in motion. Now, that air or living breath has been released in to an atmosphere, although we cannot see it clearly in the atmosphere, it will build an invisible throne to the natural eye; for the presence of God to inhabit upon. Psalms 22:3 "...but you who are holy will enthrone/inhabit in the Praises of Israel, His people. Inhabit in the Hebrew is "Yawshab" which means to sit down, to remain, to settle, or to marry. In other words, God does not merely visit us when we praise Him but He desires to have a relationship with us. When He inhabits, His presence abides and fellowships with us connecting to us as His bride. God's Spirit will dwell in our midst, take up residence and sit down on the throne of our Praise.

Let's choose the word Hallelujah to demonstrate offering up a sacrifice of praise with the fruit of our lips. Hallelujah is an expression of gratitude or adoration and is considered in the church "the highest praise." Hallelujah is one word that we can use to exhibit true praise with our lips. When we say this word, it expresses the entire realm of thanks to God. Hallelujah interjects an exclamatory thanksgiving to God who is the strong one, the creator or redeemer. Hallelujah interjects a shout out suddenly with excitement. Halal is the root from which "Hallelu-Jah" is formed (Strong's # 1984). "Hallel" in the Hebrew meaning to celebrate, to rave, to boast, to act like a madman; to make into a fool or to become clamorously foolish about our God and "YAH" means God. We praise our God saying Hallelujah, the breath of our new man is releasing a fleeting air to form a throne in the midst of our circumstance. Once we create an environment for God to live in, He will occupy and reside in our situation and every needed characteristic of God is present. Because we have allowed our breath to be released into the atmosphere that breath will build the platform/throne for God to inhabit. *(Refer to God's attributes in the beginning pages.)*

Spirit

The word "Breath" in the Vine's Expository Dictionary is defined from the word "Pneuma" and primarily denotes "The Wind, Life or Spirit." Breath refers to the Spirit which, like the wind, is invisible but powerful. Jesus said to Nicodemus in St. John 3:5-8 "...no one can enter the kingdom of God unless they are born of water and the Spirit; flesh gives birth to flesh, but the Spirit gives birth to Spirit." Jesus also told Nicodemus that he should not be surprised at his sayings that "You must be born again" of the Spirit of God. Jesus continues his explanation by saying "The wind blows wherever it pleases, you hear its sound, but you cannot tell where it comes from or where it is going; and so it is with everyone born of the Spirit."

We can also define breath, or to breathe, as air that we inhale or exhale. As we exhale praises, letting our breath praise God; we are then releasing the power of words into the atmosphere, which will build an invisible throne in our environment and God will inhabit our praises. The breath becomes a moving air carrying our words of praise and giving life to what we are speaking. There is death and life in the power of our tongue: and they that love it shall eat the fruit thereof (Proverbs 18:21). As we release praise into the atmosphere, we will give life and change to our surroundings. The word breath represents wind, breeze and movement of strength in an intangible direction as a fleeting air; and we praise, breathing words of thanksgiving. God will sit down in the midst of our situation and the sweet aroma of our praise and worship will be pleasing to Him.

God is a Spirit and they that worship Him, must worship in Spirit, even the mute can worship God. If you are mute, but redeemed, your new created man on the inside of you that God breathed into you, can breathe some hallelujahs and formulate an invisible throne in your situation also. The redeemed man on the inside of the mute man can praise and worship God too. The mute man can obtain the same results as a man that can speak words, because the spirit of God speaks through him or her. The voiceless man has the same blood brought right in praise and worship; for there is no respect of person with God (Romans 2:11). It is not you speaking, but the Spirit of your Father speaking through you (Matthew 10:20).

Cornerstones

I Peter 2:9

⁹But ye are a chosen generation, a royal priesthood, an holy nation, a peculiar people; that ye should shew forth the praises of him who hath called you out of darkness into his marvelous light

In the Biblical days, stones were commonly used for building new structures. The cornerstone had the greatest importance because it was needed to bind the sides together where the walls began; the foundation was needed to stabilize and distribute the weight of the building. Without the Cornerstone there could be no foundation; however, today, Jesus is our Cornerstone. So, we as spiritual temples being built here on earth, we must have our Chief Cornerstone, who is Jesus Christ, to bind us together and be the foundation of His spiritual temples. He will stabilize and distribute the weight of His Glory, to His chosen vessels, in order to stabilize the building of His kingdom. The distribution of His anointing upon His vessels will establish His spiritual house, so that it might be secure for this work.

In I Peter, the second chapter, we are characterized as living stones that are being built into a spiritual house. We are a holy priesthood being built into the kingdom of God, in order that we might offer spiritual sacrifices acceptable to God through Jesus Christ. We are exemplified as lively stones, chosen people, and holy priesthood and precious in the sight of God; that we may declare praise of Him who has called us out of darkness into His wonderful light. We are being built into a spiritual house here on earth, in order that God might dwell in the midst. We are to offer up spiritual sacrifices of praise and worship to God through Christ Jesus.

As Royal Priests, we should be vibrant with life wherein we are eager to serve and work in the kingdom and excited about our makeover. As a result, we should be eager and ready to do this work in the kingdom and tell of His goodness. Furthermore, we should be people that are exciting with life, energetic and enthusiastic about this assignment. We must not bring to God praise and worship that is lifeless, lethargic and sluggish, because God will not be pleased. We are a chosen priesthood, being built into a spiritual house here on earth, the Lord will dwell in the midst of us mighty. He will rejoice over us with joy, rest in His love and joy over us with singing (Zephaniah 3:17).

God spoke in His word in I Peter 2:6 that He would lay a stone in Zion, who is Jesus and He will be our Chief Cornerstone; and whoever believes in Him will never be put to shame. With Jesus, we will never be unstable, and assured to never crumble or go under (Hebrew 13:5). Jesus **guarantees** us that He will never leave us; nor forsake us; therefore, with Him we will be successful and victorious in all things because we are triumphant over-comers and more than conquerors. We must remember that the enemy that comes to kill, steal and destroy will never be able to render more strength than the God who has chosen us. Although Jesus never leaves us, we become more conscious of His presence when we Praise and Worship Him because our focus is directly upon Him.

With Jesus' guarantee, there is a testimony of security through Jesus' death, burial and resurrection power. The people of God were left a last will and testament which is covenant of His proof and loyalty. A last will and testament is a legal document declaring or expressing spoken or written words of that person's intention when he dies; the promises of God are our legal document. This type of document is typically signed in advance while in good health, however, Jesus signed this will with His Blood. Jesus' Will and Testament is the Word of God and this declaration was to the manner in which He would have His estate disposed of after his death; and that was to His Children, the children of God. The word of God is Jesus' written will.

As previously stated, the verses in the 2nd Chapter of Peter explain to us that we, as people of God, were exemplified as the living stone and His chosen people. We are precious in the sight of God and are being built into a spiritual house in order that we might be a holy priesthood offering up spiritual sacrifices to God through Christ Jesus.

We are the building stones, for the construction of the temple of God here on earth. Being lively stones, we are vibrant with life, wherein we serve; we work in this assembly as a Holy Priest, offering up Praises to God through Jesus Christ.

As we work and perform our duties in these gatherings of worship, we are to believe and trust in Jesus Christ who is the Chief Cornerstone. When we believe in Him, the word of God comforts us in saying that we will never regret or be put to shame or disappointed for choosing to trust in Him. We are chosen, picked out, and are Gods special possessions. This is what makes us jewels, precious stones in the hand of God.

In Isaiah 43:1-7, the LORD says He has created us, and formed us; and He has shaped us and fashioned us. God has molded our very character for this work in the Kingdom; therefore, we do not have to be afraid for we are in the Hand of the Most High God our Creator, who reigns over the elements, the animals and the entire heavenly armies which are in the hand of Jehovah Tseboath; the Lord Almighty, the Lord of Armies and the Lord of Host.

Isaiah prophesied that Jehovah Tsebaoth is with us and He has redeemed us from the curse of the Law. The Lord of Host has already brought us back from the slavery of sin, called us by name and engraved us in His hand. In Isaiah 43:13, God says to us, "There is no one who is able to take you out of my hand: when I undertake a thing no one can change my purpose; no one can oppose what I do. No one can reverse my actions." (NASB/NLT). Paul Quoted Isaiah in Romans 9:29 and said "If the Lord of Host who is the Lord of the heavenly Armies, Jehovah Tsebaoth had left us, all future generations would have become like and resemble Sodom and Gomorrah. For that land was covered with brimstone, salt, and burning debris; and this land was not able to either plant nor sprout nor produce grass. Nevertheless, God has not left us, He has given us a sure foundation; a Chief Cornerstone that He may plant His Chosen People, His Royal Priest, His Holy Nation, and build His people into the temple that He desires for His Kingdom.

In Roman 9:33, God said, "... I am laying in Zion a Stone..." I am laying in the Church a Chief Cornerstone and His name is Jesus – who will be your **sure** foundation. Without a doubt, we will be firm, secure and steadfast and unmovable in this Kingdom work that He Himself has assigned.

He is the God who is the light of the world and darkness cannot overcome; and He will guide our feet into the path of peace.

Stones were commonly used for building in the biblical days; they were also used as memorials of important events. They were gathered out of cultivated fields to construct the buildings. When constructing a new building; the Cornerstone was the first stone laid at the corner.

When we come together as Living Stones to form this temple here on earth and then, with the hand of God, allow Him to build us upon the Chief Cornerstone, we can be steadfast and unmovable, always abounding in the work of the Lord we are successful and victorious in this work, we are triumphant over comers and more than conquerors – that our labor will be not in vain (I Cor. 15:58); for unless the Lord builds the House, our labor is in vain.

God's people are the living stones, vibrant with life and God has favored them – to be formed into the spiritual temple here on earth with the very spirit of God dwelling in their midst.

We are precious stones in the hand of an Almighty God because we have been divinely appointed instruments to make up the spiritual temple of God. We have been constructed by the hand of God to Praise and Worship Him.

As we assemble together, praising Him for bringing us out of darkness and into His marvelous light, God compiles us as one Body of Christ and constructs us into His earthly Royal Priesthood.

We are so precious in God's sight that He told us we are protected from the destroyer and He has inscribed and engraved us in the palms of His hands; and no one can pluck or snatch us out of the mighty hand of God.

- The meaning of "Hand" in Strong's concordance #3027 – means "by which a work is accomplished;" We in the Mighty hand of God will accomplished the work that He has called us to do; for in the King's hand, the Royal Priesthood is proficient to carry out the orders given by Him and capable of completing those commands;

- Hand in the Greek – also describes "triumphant rejoicing." We are in the Mighty Hand of the Most High God, we can rejoice because we always triumph in Christ Jesus – we always win and overcome in this work.

Proclaiming the Virtues

As I studied the Scripture, in I Peter 2:9 – one of the translations read "But you are a chosen race, a royal priesthood, a holy nation, a people of His own, so that you may proclaim the **virtues** of the one who called you out of darkness into His marvelous light."

In other words, you may decree and state publicly the intrinsic worth or God's attributes. We are to make assertive declarations that Our God is good and His mercy is everlasting and His truth endured to all generations. We are to publicize God's unique Persona and qualities because He is God, the God of Covenant and what He promised us He will do.

Psalm 89:34 (King James Version)
³⁴ My covenant will I not break, nor alter the thing that is gone out of my lips –
Exodus 15:26, for I am the Lord that healeth thee, who is Jehovah Rapha, I am El Shaddai the Almighty God, the God of more than Enough

I began to study the word **virtues** and the reference scriptures that went along with this verse, I found in my study that they pointed to the **victories** that God's people obtained; it emphasized the benefits and advantages that God's people have. For when we speak of God, we can speak of his attributes and His performances, His actions and deeds; that's what Praise is. Praise is a response to His performances and what God has done, is doing and will do for us. We react with a "Thank You Jesus" and we reply with a Hallelujah, for the Goodness of our God!

A reference scripture that led me to the Proclamation of the Virtues was found in the Book of

Exodus 19:5-6 and 23:22. The virtues were the triumphant achievements that God's people attained or accomplished by the power of the Most High God because God had selected them. He had preferred them; He favored them and selected them.

When we are favored and selected by God, there will be some opposition, and although we are favored, God gave us a condition. The condition was "If You Obey Him then out of all the nations you will be my treasured possession." He goes on to say, "Out of all the nations you will be my kingdom of priest and a holy nation and I will be an enemy to your enemy and oppose those who oppose you." If we are careful to obey God and follow His instruction, He will be an adversary to your adversaries. (Exodus 23:22)

All God wants us to do is declare, say publicly, and speak out His praise, broadcasting what He has done for us; **Obey the Word of God**.

God gave us an example from the Levitical Priesthood in the Biblical days: when the priest would enter into the presence of God, offering up their prayers, thanksgiving and sacrifices he wore a breastplate with precious gems that symbolized the Garden of Eden, when man was free from sin. The priest would enter into the God's presence and make atonement for sin.

The Greek word for "breastplate" which was designed by God Himself meant "**a speaking place**" and this place of speaking was where God revealed His divine will to His chosen people.

In the breastplate worn by the High Priest were precious jewels or stones that represented the 12 tribes of Israel but, **according to the researchers** each stone in the High Priest's E-phod, had certain values.

- One of the stones was good to strengthen the heart and calms the mood;
- One was good for the cleansing of the blood;
- One was good to increase wisdom, aid in learning and bring success in business;
- One was to remove worry and fear;
- One was to strengthen the eyes and bring peace; restore memory and help one speak wise;
- One brings longevity and strengthens weak hearing;
- One could bring joy peace and happiness and repel the enemy; and
- One would prevent hemorrhaging.

However, as I read the researchers' comments, surveys, investigations and evaluations, I was reminded that instead of having to call upon each individual stone for these attributes, call on the name that is above all names; that name is Jesus, who the builders rejected. In the Book of Revelation 19:13, His name is called the Word of God, who is the Chief Cornerstone and if we trust in Him our building will never collapse. Jesus, as the foundation, will stabilize His people and distribute the weight of His Glory, so that He will be glorified. For in Him we live, move and have our being; and all the characteristics exist. The Word in St. John 1:12 became flesh and dwelt among us and as many as received Him; He gave them the right to become children of God.

Instead of looking to the individual stones, make our request known unto the Chief Cornerstone that will meet all our needs according to His riches in Glory; and the peace of God that surpasses all understanding will keep our hearts and minds through Christ Jesus (Philippians 4:19). For without this stone we will be like the useless stones as in Jeremiah 51 and there would be no use to evaluate and investigate because without the sure foundation; our existence would crumble.

It is a reality and an actuality that the Stone that the builders rejected has shaped us and formed us in his hand for His kingdom work here on earth and no individual stone is equal or can even compare to the Cornerstone; because all of the attributes found in the individual stones are found in the Keystone who is Jesus, the Matchless Lamb of God.

We are the living stone and chosen to declare the praises of Him who has brought us out of darkness and translated us into the Kingdom of His dear Son (Jesus Christ).

Praise Him because:

- He changed us;
- He converted us;
- He transformed us;
- He made us over; and
- He has repaired and restored our hearts, minds and soul out of darkness.

He has brought us out of Darkness:

- Out of the Blindness that had us ignorant to the divine things of God; and

- Out of the wickedness of sin, idolatry and sexual immorality that we once practiced and walked in.

He promised us in Isaiah 43:2-21:

- When you go through the waters of life, remember they will not overwhelm you for I am with you;
- When you walk through the fires of life you will not be burned and the flames will not harm you, for I am with you;
- When you go through deep waters and great trouble, I will be with you. So be not dismayed;
- When you go through rivers of difficulty and the complexity and the complication tend to take you under, Remember, you will not drown! For I am the Lord of Host and I am with you;
- When you walk through the fire of oppression and the harshness and cruelty of this life seems to devour you, you will not be burned up; the flames will not consume you;
- When it seems like you are in over your head- and the waters are about to drown you, and the enemy comes in like a flood, I will lift up a standard against Him;
- When you are between the rock and a hard place, it won't be a dead end, because I am with you;
- For I am the Lord thy God, the Holy One of Israel, your savior and you are precious in my sight, you are a precious jewel in my

- I have you in my hand and no man can pluck you out – I have engraved you in the palm of my hand and when I bless you no one can reverse it; and
- For I am Jehovah Tsebaoth, the Lord of Host, The angel, element, animal and the earth obeys me, you are precious in my sight and I love you. I am God and when I act nobody can reverse it.

When we are favored and selected by God, there will be some opposition, but the Lord assures us in His word "I will be an enemy to your enemy and oppose those who oppose, because you are favored and precious stones in my sight."

He assures us in His word that "I've got you in my hand and no man can pluck you out, No man can reverse what I've called for you, because You have been engraved/inscribed the hand of the Most High God. In My Mighty Hand, you will accomplish the Work that I've called you to do." The Weapons may form, but will not prosper. Just put on the Whole armor of God that you might be able to stand against the wiles of the devil and when you've done all you can, just stand.

El Shadai/El Shadday is the Breasty One who nourishes and supplies all our needs. He is all bountiful, all sufficient and has chosen His Royal Priesthood to speak and sing of His Goodness, revealing His divine will for the kingdom. He has placed His Priest in a position that He might use them as instruments to speak through, speaking forth His purpose and plans on earth.

Embraced in His Love – Enveloped in His Glory and Endued with His Power

I Peter 2:9

⁹ But ye are a chosen generation, a royal priesthood, an holy nation, a peculiar people; that ye should shew forth the praises of him who hath called you out of darkness into his marvellous light

For the Kingdom here on earth, God has chosen the people of God to be a holy priesthood, offering up spiritual sacrifices of Praise to Him through Christ Jesus.

As Royal priests, we should be vibrant with life wherein we are eager to serve and work in the kingdom and excited about our makeover. As a result, we should be eager and ready to do this work in the kingdom and tell of His goodness. Furthermore, we should be people that are exciting with life, energetic and enthusiastic about this assignment. We must not bring to God praise and worship that is lifeless, lethargic and sluggish, because God will not be pleased. Since we are a chosen priesthood, being built into a spiritual house here on earth, the Lord will dwell in the midst of us mightily. He will rejoice over us with joy, rest in His love and joy over us with singing (Zephaniah 3:17).

In the Biblical days, stones were commonly used for building new structures; and the cornerstone had the greatest importance because it was needed to bind together the sides where the walls began. Without the cornerstone, there could be no ground work. Without a cornerstone, there could be no foundation in order to stabilize and distribute the weight of the building. So, for the spiritual temples to be built and stable, God, our Father, laid a Stone in Zion who will be our Chief Cornerstone and His name is Jesus and we are guaranteed to never crumble or go under because "I Am" is with us always. He will never leave us; nor forsake us.

Stones were commonly used for building in the biblical days; they were also used as memorials of important events. They were gathered out of cultivated fields to construct the buildings. Stones are made from pressure and age and we in the hand of the Almighty God have been prepared for this work of the Kingdom through the pressures of life. However, we are considered genuine because we have outlasted the suffering. The more pressure and the hotter the temperatures of life, the more expensive, costly or genuine is the stone.

For a **diamond** to become genuine it must go through an extreme heating process until it is colorless and flawless. This gem is crushed and baked onto a cutting tool. The more this gem goes through the heating process, the purer it becomes and the more valuable it turns out to be. An **imitation diamond** is softer and shows scratches, signs of wear and tear and does not have the fortitude to survive the process that a true gem does.

When we, as Living Stones, go through the heated pressures of life, through stress, anxiety, demand and difficulties, we then have begun the process that transforms us into the precious stones that God has called for such a time as now. These are the times when God is shaping and molding us into the valuable stones for His Kingdom. Through many of these experiences, when completed, we will come out purified and priceless in the Hand of God.

Of all the stones, the cornerstone had the greatest importance because it was needed to bind together the sides, where the walls began. When constructing a new building, the cornerstone was the first stone laid at the corner. The cornerstone was the joining stone and without the cornerstone there could be no underpinning or no establishment for this was the keystone that locked the others stones in place. The keystone is the stone that the other stones depends on to secure the building.

When God brings us together as Living Stones to form this temple here on earth; the mighty hand of God builds us upon the Chief Cornerstone, who is Jesus Christ. We then and only then are steadfast and unmovable, always abounding in the work of the Lord. We, as royal priesthood, are successful and victorious in this work; triumphant over-comers and more than conquerors; then our labor will be not in vain (I Corinthians 15:58).

God promised us in Psalm 89:34 (KJV), "My covenant will I not break, nor alter the thing that is gone out of my lips." He also promised us in Exodus 15:26, "...for I am the Lord that healeth thee." Jehovah Rapha/Ropheka is the Lord that heals us. He told us that He is El Shaddai/El Shadday the Almighty God, the God of more than enough (Genesis 17:1). "El" signifies Strong One and Shaddai/Shadday signifies "The Breasty One." This name pictures God as the Strong Nourisher, Strength Giver, Satisfier and all Bountiful, the Supplier of the needs of His people. Therefore, He is well able to build us into His Temple to represent Him in His Kingdom.

The priest in the Biblical days entered into the God's presence and made atonement for the sins of the people. When they enter into the presence of God, offering up their prayers, thanksgiving and sacrifices;

they wore a breastplate with precious gems that symbolized the Garden of Eden when man was free from sin. The Greek word for "Breastplate" which was designed by God Himself meant "a speaking place;" and this place of speaking was where God revealed His divine will to His chosen people. Within the breastplate worn by the High Priest, were precious jewels or stones that represented the 12 tribes of Israel and the Ephod was part of the attire which was an embroidered garment, believed to be like an apron with shoulder straps.

We are the living stone and chosen to declare the praises of Him who has brought us out of darkness and translated us into the Kingdom of His Dear Son, who is Jesus Christ. We are chosen to praise Him because He changed and made us over; He repaired and restored our hearts, minds and soul out of darkness. He has transformed us out of the blindness that had us ignorant to the divine things of God. He has converted us out of the wickedness of sin, idolatry and sexual immorality that we once practiced and walked in. Therefore, we are to declare publicly what He has done.

God has promised us in Isaiah 43:2-21 that when you go through the waters of life, remember they will not overwhelm you for He is with us. When you walk through the fires of life you will not be burned and the flames will not harm you, for He is with us. When you go through deep waters and great trouble, to not be not dismayed for the Lord will take care of us. When you go through rivers of difficulty and the complexity and the complication tend to take you under, remember, we will not drown; for the Lord of Host is with us. When you walk through the fire of oppression and the harshness and cruelties of this life seem to devour you, you will not be consumed. When it seems like the waters of life are over your head and you are about to drown, God will lift up a standard against the enemy. When you are between the rock and a hard place, it will not be a dead end, because God is with us and He is more that the whole world against us. The Lord our God, the Holy One of Israel, our Savior will never leave us nor forsake us and we are precious jewels in His sight.

By faith we have been guaranteed the promises because we are Abraham's offspring. God has set his seal of ownership upon us and put his Spirit in our hearts; therefore, we are guaranteed what is to come. We can praise and worship God because He has deposited a guaranteed inheritance until the day of redemption. Christ has set His seal of ownership on us and we have been guaranteed our inheritance by His Blood.

God has formed us from Himself that we might show forth His Praise (Isa 43:21). Therefore, we must **"Be"** Praise and Worshippers, rather than just **"Do"** Praise and Worship. Usually, when we "Do" praise and worship, we perform and complete the task as a duty rather than expressing our genuine love and thanks to God. To **"Be"** Praise and Worshippers one should have a heart that worship's God and an attitude that loves God in spite of what He blesses us with; a worshiper worships God just because He is God.

As a reminder, when we praise God, we must enter into His gates with thanksgiving, responding to His actions and deeds that have been performed in our lives. When we Worship, We must enter into the Presence of God responding to Him as Lord, Majesty and King. Our behavior should result in the reply, to obeying His Word. When we respond to His presence with "We worship you Lord;" we are making known that He has the authority over us and everything we are, do and have. When we respond to His presence with "We worship our King;" we are proclaiming that God is the principle piece of our lives and is number one in importance. When we respond to His presence with "We worship our Majesty," we are saying publicly, that God's reigning influence rules our entire existence. If His word says, "to offer up a sacrifice of praise to God continually, that is, the fruit of our lips giving thanks to his name" (Hebrews 13:15), then we should obey. We should find ourselves obeying the instructions in God's word because we love Him.

All scripture is given by inspiration of God, and is profitable for doctrine, for reproof, for correction, for instruction in righteousness, so we may be perfect, thoroughly furnished unto all good works. (II Timothy 3:16-17). As we enter into God's presence, we should go in with our view and vision tunneled upon Christ; thanking him for what He has done and who He is. We should tunnel our spiritual vision on the Lord Jesus; lifting up our hands in obedience, offering up a sacrifice of praise with the fruit of our lips thanking God. He will then enthrone on our praises. When He enthrones on our praises, He will, bring with Him all of His characteristics. Whatever we need, God has it and is willing to provide for the need. As we are entering into His presences, we are letting our voice of praise be heard, clapping our hands and shouting unto God with a voice of triumph because we already have the victory over every situation. We are shouting and clapping because we have an assurance that we are more than conquerors.

To clap expresses approval and is an emphatic expression of joy. Psalms 47:1 says: "Clap your hands, all you peoples; shout to God with loud songs of joy" (NRSV). As we enter the presence of God, clapping our hands, we are as instruments expressing delight and excitement. In the Hebrew, to "clap" (Taqa) means to clatter, to clang, and is often described as blowing a trumpet or sounding the alarm. It indicates energy and enthusiasm. Therefore, as we clap our hands in obedience to the Word and shout, which is sudden outburst, we will automatically send forth our ministering spirit (Hebrew 1:14) and the battle is won. We are kings and priests, and a King clapped his hands in order to call for his servant. When we clap our hands when Praising God, we are also calling for our servants, who are the angels that have charge over us, to perform the necessary need. II Chronicles 20:17 reminds us, "Ye shall not need to fight in this battle, set yourselves, stand ye still and see the salvation of the Lord with us...." Thus, praise and worship is one of the weapons of our warfare for the Kingdom of God for once we Obey the Word of God, God will do the rest.

Our mindset and posture should be totally focused on the Calvary experience, remembering that praise and worship is not for entertainment purposes. In Isaiah 5:11-12, we notice a "woe" to entertainers who performed the duties of worship, but whose hearts were far from true worship. These entertainers did not respect the work of the Lord; nor did they consider the cleanness of their hands as they operated.

> *Isaiah 5:11-12 (KJV)*
>
> [11] *Woe unto them that rise up early in the morning, that they may follow strong drink; that continue until night, till wine inflame them!*
>
> [12] *And the harp, and the viol, the tabret, and pipe, and wine, are in their feasts: but they regard not the work of the LORD, neither consider the operation of his hands.*

Lucifer was an anointed cherub created for worship until pride got him cast out of heaven (Isaiah 14:12-15). We must be genuine praise and worshippers, laying all pride and self-righteousness aside. The Father only seeks true worshippers to be intimate with (St. John 4:23); therefore, we must not allow the flesh to be on exhibit in His presence, because this will manifest a spirit of entertainment. The word of God tells us that "No Flesh should glory in His Presence and No Flesh will be justified in His sight," (I Corinthians 1:29 and Romans 3:20). Therefore, we must not allow our worship to become entertainment for the people in the audience. We must die to the fleshly actions and realize God is the only one we should be focused on when we are worshipping. The old nature is an enmity against God and does not desire to humble itself in His presence, consequently, the flesh will try to receive the credit for the presence of God manifesting (Romans 6:11 and Romans 8:6-8). The only one we should be addressing is the Almighty God and viewing Him as the only one in the congregation watching and listening to our worship. Remembering our entire worship experience should be directed toward and to God, our creator.

God laid out a plan where we can come into His presence and tangibly feel His Glory overshadow us. God's layout plan will help us understand the procedures when entering into His presence. As we study the plan and create the atmosphere, God will enthrone on our praises. The Old Testament had regulations for worship in the tabernacle and I believe this was a plan to exemplify a procedure for us today in order to enter into God's presence. Since we are a Holy Priesthood acceptable to God by the Blood of Jesus Christ, we now have access to the entry key and eligibility to enter into the face of God.

Hebrews 9:12 (KJV)

[12] Neither by the blood of goats and calves, but by his own blood he entered in once into the holy place, having obtained eternal redemption for us.

Hebrews 10:19 (KJV)

[19] Having therefore, brethren, boldness to enter into the holiest by the blood of Jesus

Exodus 25:40 (KJV)

[40] And look that thou make them after their pattern, which was shewed thee in the mount.

At the beginning of our new lives in Christ, we were given all of the reproductive organs of worship in order to produce for the Kingdom; because we must commence the reproductive process for the Kingdom through worship. However, sin has caused us to be sterile; therefore, we must repent, and then yield to God for healing and restoration in order to become fertile again. Some of us have become barren from unrepentant sin, but I believe God is still in the forgiving business if we humble ourselves and turn from our wicked ways. He will give us a brand new start. Since we have declined to obey in worship, our reproductive system has shut down, but in spite of all, God is able to do exceedingly abundant above all that we ask or think, according to the power that works in us (Eph. 3:20).

I believe the Bride of Christ, who is the Body of Christ, is in a period of ovulation and is fertile and ready to produce for the Kingdom; however, sin can cause God's people to be infertile and incapable of producing. Sin can cause us to be powerless, weak, impotent and even useless to multiply and produce for the Kingdom. Sin can cause sterilization and, furthermore, cause the Body of Christ to become barren where we will have no eggs to produce or release into the kingdom. I believe when we worship we release from our spiritual womb eggs or seeds of worship and we as the Bride of Christ carry in our spiritual fetus Kingdom offspring that must be birthed into the earth for such a time as now. Once we begin to worship in Spirit and in Truth, these eggs of worship are released and unite with the Holy Spirit and Jesus, who is Truth, causing the spiritual womb to become fertile. That embryo will continue to develop until birthed into the kingdom here on earth.

Some individual and corporate worshippers will have a few problems bringing forth God's purposes and plans because the traditions of men have tied some of their tubes. In the Book of Colossians, chapter 2, verse 8, we are warned to be careful not to allow anyone to captivate us through deceptive philosophy, which depends on human tradition and the basic principles of this world rather than on Christ. As well, some of their eggs are old and in a stage of Down Syndrome because they have not released eggs of worship in such a long time that the worship has become abnormal and undeveloped. When one releases an egg of worship that is in a stage of Down Syndrome, they can only birth confusion, chaos and disorder into the kingdom of God. When our praise and worship is undeveloped, we have become stagnant and simply decline to obey the instructions given, having the need to be taught the truth about praise and worship. Afterward, be doers of the Word and not hearers only.

The Word of God instructs us to "Let everything that hath breath, Praise Ye the Lord;" this is an instruction that we should not forbid. When we "let" our breath praise God, we are choosing to obey those instructions. Once we have let our Breath transmit the life of God's creation into the atmosphere, as it spreads out, it will build a throne in the midst where we are worshipping. The Greek word for Breath is pnoe, which means spirit, to blow, the breath of life, wind or a movement of air. A good example of what is happening in the spiritual realm when we breathe out praises or exhale out hallelujahs is a fog or a moving air that will assemble an invisible throne right in our midst. If a person blows in their hand they can feel the effect of wind or air movement. If a person exhales onto a mirror a fog develops which shows the effects of an invisible fog that can be formed during praise and worship; and upon this invisible fog, God will inhabit. God's presence and this experience of praise and worship can bring about a change in our situation and, as a result, has the ability to build this same invisible throne where we are worshipping. Once we let our breath transmit the life of God in us; out and into the atmosphere, the breath of God will spread out, building a throne where and while we are worshipping.

As we Obey the Word of God in Psalms 150:6 and "Let everything that hath breath praise ye the Lord" speaking forth Praise out of our mouths, the Glory of God will fill the temple. Even a person who is mute can open their mouth and allow your breath to breathe praise into the atmosphere and God will inhabit on the throne of their praise and worship. We actually build a throne with praise and worship in God's presence.

Psalms 50:23 teaches that "Whosoever offereth praise glorifieth me, and to him that ordereth his conversation is right I will show the salvation." To offer means to present your praise to God with the aim of being accepted or rejected and defective praise is unacceptable. Defective praise is undesirable in the presence of God because it is deficient in Spirit and Truth. More often than not, when we are lacking the fullness of the Holy Ghost and have not accepted Jesus as our Lord and Savior, it is usually the cause of the absence of the Spirit and Truth. Jesus is the way into the Presence of God and His character in us is the reason we can come unto God genuinely. Jesus is the new life in us and the Holy Spirit is the power that leads us and guides us into the position which qualifies us to be in God's presence. The Father in heaven seeks out real or unadulterated worshippers and when we worship in Spirit and Truth, we imitate the actual features of Jesus and the Holy Spirit. However, if we are not saved and filled with God's Spirit it is impossible to reproduce True Praise and Worship. Matter of fact, God is omniscient and knows if we are faking true worship, therefore it is not acceptable in His sight.

The all wise God has the universal knowledge and infinitely knows all things. A God that knows all things and is endless in wisdom cannot be fooled by false praise and worship. When the presence of God inhabits, He seeks Himself within us and the True Spirit in us will draw unto God. So, as we show forth our praise as an act toward our God, we honor and give the reverence that is due our creator. We should continually order and command our sentiments toward God and regulate our verbal exchange to Him then He will manifest His saving power in our midst. As we lift up our Holy hand in the sanctuary and bless the Names of Jesus, commanding the fruit of our lips to praise Him with a heart of repentance, taking control over our flesh and brining it under subjection in worship, God will inhabit. True Praise and Worshippers love to Obey God's instructions.

Instructions for Offering Praise and Worship

Command your entire being to praise and worship God.

We as Christians have been instructed to praise and worship God. The Soul is in a process of being renewed day by day and our bodies will be made new. However, while we are here on the earth, the soul and body functions together as the Flesh. The Flesh is considered our sinful nature and we must not live under the control of our sinful nature. The sinful nature is at war with God and does not obey the instructions of God therefore, we must live under the control of the Holy Spirit, who will command our entire being to praise and worship God.

Romans 8:5-7 NIV

⁵ Those who live according to the flesh have their minds set on what the flesh desires; but those who live in accordance with the Spirit have their minds set on what the Spirit desires. 6 The mind governed by the flesh is death, but the mind governed by the Spirit is life and peace.

⁷ The mind governed by the flesh is hostile to God; it does not submit to God's law, nor can it do so.

⁸ Those who are in the realm of the flesh cannot please God.

Scriptures to Obey that refer to Praising and Worshipping God with our entire being:

Hands

Psalm 134:2

² *Lift up your hands in the sanctuary, and bless the LORD.*

Psalm 63:4

⁴ *Thus will I bless thee while I live: I will lift up my hands in thy name.*

Psalm 47:1

¹ *O clap your hands, all ye people; shout unto God with the voice of triumph.*

Head

Psalm 24:7

⁷ *Lift up your heads, O ye gates; and be ye lift up, ye everlasting doors; and the King of glory shall come in.*

Psalm 24:9

⁹ *Lift up your heads, O ye gates; even lift them up, ye everlasting doors; and the King of glory shall come in*

Psalm 138:2

² *I will worship toward thy holy temple, and praise thy name for thy lovingkindness and for thy truth: for thou hast magnified thy word above all thy name.*

Voice

Psalm 66:8

⁸ *O bless our God, ye people, and make the voice of his praise to be heard:*

Psalm 98:4-5

⁴ Make a joyful noise unto the LORD, all the earth: make a loud noise, and rejoice, and sing praise.

⁵ Sing unto the LORD with the harp; with the harp, and the voice of a psalm.

Luke 19:37

³⁷ And when he was come nigh, even now at the descent of the mount of Olives, the whole multitude of the disciples began to rejoice and praise God with a loud voice for all the mighty works that they had seen;

Lips, Mouth, Tongue

Psalm 63:3

³ Because thy loving kindness is better than life, my lips shall praise thee.

Psalms 63:5

⁵ My soul shall be satisfied as with marrow and fatness; and my mouth shall praise thee with joyful lips:

Psalm 71:8

⁸ Let my mouth be filled with thy praise and with thy honour all the day.

Psalm 71:23-24

²³ My lips shall greatly rejoice when I sing unto thee; and my soul, which thou hast redeemed.

²⁴ My tongue also shall talk of thy righteousness all the day long: for they are confounded, for they are brought unto shame, that seek my hurt.

Psalm 109:30

30 I will greatly praise the LORD with my mouth; yea, I will praise him among the multitude.

Psalm 145:21

21 My mouth shall speak the praise of the LORD: and let all flesh bless his holy name for ever and ever

Mind/Soul

Psalm 104:34

34 My meditation of him shall be sweet: I will be glad in the LORD.

Psalm 6:5

5 For in death there is no remembrance of thee: in the grave who shall give thee thanks?

Psalm 146:1

1 Praise ye the LORD. Praise the LORD, O my soul.

Psalm 86:2

2 Preserve my soul; for I am holy: O thou my God, save thy servant that trusteth in thee.

Psalms 103:2

2 Bless the LORD, O my soul, and forget not all his benefits

Feet

Psalm 149:3

³ Let them praise his name in the dance: let them sing praises unto him with the timbrel and harp.

Psalm 150:4

⁴ Praise him with the timbrel and dance: praise him with stringed instruments and organs.

Ecclesiastes 3:4

⁴ A time to weep, and a time to laugh; a time to mourn, and a time to dance;

2 Samuel 6:14

¹⁴ And David danced before the LORD with all his might; and David was girded with a linen ephod.

Psalm 30:11

¹¹ Thou hast turned for me my mourning into dancing: thou hast put off my sackcloth, and girded me with gladness;

Heart

Psalm 28:7

⁷ The LORD is my strength and my shield; my heart trusted in him, and I am helped: therefore my heart greatly rejoiceth; and with my song will I praise him.

Psalm 108:1

¹ O God, my heart is fixed; I will sing and give praise, even with my glory.

Psalm 9:1

¹ *I will praise thee, O LORD, with my whole heart; I will shew forth all thy marvellous works.*

Psalm 111:1

¹ *Praise ye the LORD. I will praise the LORD with my whole heart, in the assembly of the upright, and in the congregation*

Judges 5:9

⁹ *My heart is toward the governors of Israel, that offered themselves willingly among the people. Bless ye the LORD.*

Flesh

Psalm 103:1

¹ *Bless the LORD, O my soul: and all that is within me, bless his holy name.*

Psalms 145:21

²¹ *My mouth shall speak the praise of the LORD: and let all flesh bless his holy name for ever and ever*

Instruments

Psalm 150:3-4

³ *Praise him with the sound of the trumpet: praise him with the psaltery and harp.*

⁴ *Praise him with the timbrel and dance: praise him with stringed instruments and organs*

1 Chronicles 23:5

⁵ Moreover four thousand were porters; and four thousand praised the LORD with the instruments which I made, said David, to praise therewith.

Psalm 33:2

² Praise the LORD with harp: sing unto him with the psaltery and an instrument of ten strings

Psalm 149:3

³ Let them praise his name in the dance: let them sing praises unto him with the timbrel and harp.

2 Chronicles 5:13

¹³ It came even to pass, as the trumpeters and singers were as one, to make one sound to be heard in praising and thanking the LORD; and when they lifted up their voice with the trumpets and cymbals and instruments of musick, and praised the LORD, saying, For he is good; for his mercy endureth for ever: that then the house was filled with a cloud, even the house of the LORD;

Psalm 147:7

⁷ Sing unto the LORD with thanksgiving; sing praise upon the harp unto our God:

2 Chronicles 30:21

²¹ And the children of Israel that were present at Jerusalem kept the feast of unleavened bread seven days with great gladness: and the Levites and the priests praised the LORD day by day, singing with loud instruments unto the LORD.

Psalm 144:9

⁹ *I will sing a new song unto thee, O God: upon a psaltery and an instrument of ten strings will I sing praises unto thee.*

2 Chronicles 7:6

⁶ *And the priests waited on their offices: the Levites also with instruments of musick of the LORD, which David the king had made to praise the LORD, because his mercy endureth for ever, when David praised by their ministry; and the priests sounded trumpets before them, and all Israel stood*

Psalm 71:22

²² *I will also praise thee with the psaltery, even thy truth, O my God: unto thee will I sing with the harp, O thou Holy One of Israel.*

Isaiah 38:20

²⁰ *The LORD was ready to save me: therefore we will sing my songs to the stringed instruments all the days of our life in the house of the LORD.*

2 Chronicles 29:27

²⁷ *And Hezekiah commanded to offer the burnt offering upon the altar. And when the burnt offering began, the song of the LORD began also with the trumpets, and with the instruments ordained by David king of Israel.*

Psalm 33:3

³ *Sing unto him a new song; play skillfully with a loud noise.*

Command Them to Praise,
They are Subject to the Holy Spirit in You

- Lips, you will praise;
- Head, you will look toward the Hills whence comes your help;
- Feet, you will dance;
- Hand, you will clap and surrender to the Most High God;
- Body, you will serve with gladness;
- Mind, you are brought under subjection to the Calvary Experience and tunneling your vision upon Jesus Christ our Lord.

Hebrews 9:18 teaches that the first covenant was established with blood and when Moses had spoken every command to all the people according to the law, he took the blood of calves and goats with water and scarlet wool and hyssop and sprinkled both the book itself and all the people. Likewise, Moses sprinkled with blood all of the tabernacle and the utensils of worship. According to the Law, everything was cleansed with blood, for without the shedding of blood there was no forgiveness (Hebrew 9:18).

Christ entered into heaven itself and now appears in God's presence for us. He did not have to enter himself again and again as the High Priest in the Old Testament entered the sanctuary year after year with blood which was not their own. Jesus came as the High Priest by a greater and more perfect tabernacle, which was not made with hands. Jesus appeared once, for all, and concluded and completed the assignment that God the Father sent Him to do, which was to redeem His people back from the curse of the Law. He put away sin by His sacrifice. Christ was offered once to bear the sins of many and bring about salvation. We are the temples of the Holy Ghost which is in us and the Spirit of God dwells in us. The Tabernacle diagram will help us to understand the method when entering into God's presence.

The Tabernacle is a prototype of heaven and is God's laid out diagram for us to follow when entering His Presence. This diagram will map out the route into the Holy of Holies, so that praise and worship leaders can easily set the atmosphere when invoking the presence of God. As we follow this map and the procedures to enter into the Holy of Holies, God will enthrone upon the praises of His people. (Psalms 22:3, "... but thou are holy, Oh thou that inhabits the praise of Israel."

We are the Royal Priesthood, a holy nation, a people of His own chosen by God; we have access to use the entry key and are eligible to enter in freely by the Blood of Jesus Christ. We will enter into God's presence and proclaim the excellences and goodness of Him who has called us out of darkness into His marvelous light (I Peter 2:9).

Before Christ, the only access to God was through the earthly High Priest, who would offer a sacrifice by using the animal's blood to first cover his own sins and then the sins of the people. Thanks be to God the Father, for the sacrifice of Christ once, for all. His blood made atonement and restored us from the fall of Adam.

God wanted to dwell among His people and have fellowship with them, therefore, He commanded Moses to build a tabernacle. As we study the tabernacle, we understand God's pattern of worship. The tabernacle was a shadow of things in heaven and also a foreshadow of the redemptive work of Jesus Christ. The real tabernacle is in heaven where Jesus Himself is our high priest.

We are the royal priesthood, a peculiar people and a holy nation; and our bodies are the temples of the Holy Ghost. God has called us out of darkness and into His marvelous light, so we should show forth praises. As we follow the pattern of worship, entering into the presence of God by the Blood of Jesus who is the High priest, let us look unto Jesus the author and finisher of our faith (Hebrew 12:2).

Class Exercise:

In the previous chapters the instructions were given in regards to Praise and Worship. As we prepare to implement the Praise and Worship experience, we will demonstrate and exhibit praise and worship through this exercise.

Let us exhibit and actually praise and worship as we enter into God's presences, entering His gates with thanksgiving and into His courts with praise. We will begin to thank Him and bless His name for He is good, His mercy is everlasting and His truth endures through all generations. Let us enter into God's presence lifting up our hands and voices in a sound of praise, while communicating and conveying our love to God and touching Him with our Worship.

Demonstration and Procedures When We Enter into the Holy of Holies

The Posture or the Attitude for genuine Praise and Worship entering into the Gates and the Court grounds

In one translation of Hebrews 8:5, Moses was instructed at Mt. Sinai to make the tabernacle that was based upon the heavenly pattern shown to him and in Exodus 25:40 the tabernacle was a replica of the heavens. Hebrews 8:5 of the New King James Version it says, "Who serve unto the copy and shadow of heavenly things, as Moses was divinely instructed when he was about to make the tabernacle. For He said, "See that you make all things according to the pattern shown you on the mountain."

Therefore, this prototype of heaven gives us an example of the format when entering into the Holy of Holies. As we enter into God's presence, visualizing this format, we should picture step by step each piece of the furniture and what they represent biblically. When we come into the presence of God, acknowledging and appreciating Him, each piece of the furniture in the tabernacle reveals a type of Christ.

The tabernacle reveals the key elements in God's plan of Salvation. Each piece of furniture displays the historical occurrences of what God sent Jesus to do and this study will unfold each reason for the pieces of furniture. God's plan in Hebrews 9:12 lets us know, it was neither by the blood of goats and calves but that it was by Jesus own blood that He entered into the Holy Place and obtained eternal redemption for us. So, as we enter into God's presence, we should be thanking

God for providing Jesus, the last Lamb that was slain, and the one who purchased our Salvation that we might have a right to the tree of life and the approval to enter into the Holy of Holies. We should enter into the presence of God in a posture of praise and worship, that is, with a pure heart and lifted hands.

> *Refer to Photographs of Interest section beginning on page 119: The Tabernacle*

Lamentations 3:40-41 instructs us to first search and try our ways and then turn to the Lord, then, lift up our hearts along with our hands unto God in the heavens. Lifting our hands and hearts to God is a form of repentance, as well as the attitude and posture for praise and worship. When we lift our hearts with our hands, unto God in the heavens, the inner attitude should be joined to the external act of the lifting of our hands. The hands are just an external action of what is going on internally.

The psalmist David is a good example of the approach and that was, "Search me, O God and know my heart, try me and know my thought..." (Psalms 139:23). So, our inner hearts should have repented and in the frame of mind that we love the Lord with all our heart, soul, mind and strength; and at the same time, expressing a Godly remorse for any sin that we have committed. Once we are regretful and truly sorry for sin, it will work repentance in our walk. Saying, Lord, I acknowledge my sin unto thee, and my iniquity have I not hid and I confess my transgression unto the Lord and you will forgive the iniquity of my sin (Psalms 32:5). We must yield our wills to the Lord, communicating to God that we will no longer resist the Holy Ghost that will lead us and guide us into all truths. Also, the lifting of our hand articulates a form of submitting and as we submit to God's will and no longer our will, we will be able to yield under the Glory Presence of God. Worship is the ground for intimacy and as we yield under the Glory, we are then in a position to become pregnant with the things of God in order to birth them into His Kingdom here on earth.

Matthew 25 is a parable of the Wise and Foolish Virgins and this parable is associated with the Church and with being the Bride of Christ and Christ being the bridegroom. We must understand that intimacy is a basic factor to consummate the marriage and intimacy is a key point in a union of the Bride and Groom. With intimacy God instructed Adam and Eve in Genesis 1:28 to be fruitful and multiply and replenish the earth. We, the Church, are the Bride of Christ and I believe God wants to be intimate with His bride so that we can be fruitful and multiply; and replenish the Kingdom of God with His plans and purposes here on earth.

I believe we are in a period of Ovulation as the Body of Christ and are fertile and ready to produce for the Kingdom. We, as the bride, are at the most suitable stage to birth God's plans and purposes into His kingdom; and worship is the groundwork for intimacy. As we are worshipping, the spiritual reproductive egg will be released. As we worship, this spiritual reproductive egg is released and it will unite with the semen of Spirit and Truth, impregnating us with the things of God to birth into the kingdom here on earth. When Mary, the Mother of Jesus, simply praised and worshipped God and showed her gratitude, reverence and thanks; the Power of the Highest overshadowed her impregnating her with the Holy Seed of God, who was Jesus Christ. I believe as we present true worship to God, the same Power of the Highest will overshadow us, planting into our spiritual wombs the Holy Seed of God's purposes and plans for His Kingdom. As we have prayed for God's Kingdom to come on earth as it is in Heaven, worship is foundation to establish the King of Kings domain here on earth.

Praising God gains his attention and once He is aware that we are focusing on Him, He notices us and then our praise causes us to become attractive and appealing to our God; then He will inhabit our praise (Psalm 22:3). Praise is considered the stimulating factor and the invitation for God's Glory to manifest. We understand that God never leaves us nor forsakes us, but we become more conscious of His presence when we Praise Him. When we began to Praise and Worship God, His Glory will come sit in our midst, dwell with us and even abode, then marry us; and as the marriage is consummated, some relations or intimacy will happen.

God only gets intimate with true worshippers and not those that are lifeless, dead or unresponsive entities; for God is alive and well. Any praise and worship that is defective is unacceptable because it is deficient in Spirit and in Truth. We are instructed to worship in Spirit and in Truth because our Father seeks those who worship in Spirit and Truth. The presence of God is not revealed to the world which is blinded by disobedience. In the teachings on the Holy Spirit in St. John 14:17, the word of God explains to us that the world does not see the Holy Spirit nor does it know Him because He does not reside in them. However, we know Him because He lives with us and will be in us. The Holy Spirit leads and guides His people into all truths. II Corinthians 4:4 lets us know that the god of this world has blinded the minds of those who do not believe and they cannot see the light of the good news of Christ's glory (NIV). We must understand that all that is in the world is the desires of the flesh, the desires of the eyes and the pride of life, so only when we worship God in Spirit and in Truth do we recognize His presence when His Glory fills the temple.

Proverbs 20:27 says "The Spirit of a man is the candle of the Lord, searching all the inward parts of the belly." In other words, our spirit is God's contact point, through which He lights up man and when we begin to praise God in Spirit, our candle is lit, for Him to see us in the assembly. Praise will bring God into our presence, but worship will carry us into the presence of God. So, as we draw nigh to God, He will draw nigh to us, allowing His Spirit to hover over us as He did Mary, the mother of Jesus, and impregnating us with the purposes and plan for such a time as now, to birth into the Kingdom. As we yield in worshipping in Spirit and Truth, the consuming power of the Holy Spirit will impart His purpose and plans in us to achieve the goals for His Kingdom.

Remembering that the old way of worship was set aside or superseded when, at Christ's death, the curtain of the temple was torn in two, from top to bottom (Mat 27:51). Yet, the beauty and grandeur (magnificent Glory) of the tabernacle points to the transcendent (beyond comprehension) beauty of the living God as revealed now in Jesus Christ.

I strongly suggest you study Ephesians 5:17-21, to understand our God's will and what His word instructs us to do in praise and worship; because these instructions will help us to be pure when entering into God's Presence and you will be able to clearly hear the voice of God. When we are full and overflowing with the power of the Holy Spirit it leaves no space for the flesh to maneuver or operate. At the same time make sure you are filled with the Spirit by speaking forth the Psalms; singing hymns and spiritual songs; while you are making melody in your heart. Submit to God and yield your will, so that your flesh will come subject to your spirit man.

Then enter **His gates** with thanksgiving and into his courts with praise, being thankful unto Him and blessing His name for His goodness and mercy that endures forever (Psalms 100:4).

> *Refer to Photographs of Interest section beginning on page 119: The Tabernacle (view from above).*

As we are entering into the presence of the Most High King, vocalize your love and convey your praise and worship openly, using the suggested Hebrews words described previously. The pieces of furniture symbolize and express Christ our Messiah and why we have reason to praise Him.

As we are entering progressively into the presence of God, we must visualize each piece of furniture which represents Christ and His death, burial and resurrection for us.

- We must keep our spiritual vision tunneled toward the face of God, seeking His face and not His hand while at the same time visualizing the entire Calvary experience.
- Lift up your hands with a heart of worship toward the hill from which comes your help (Psalms 134:2), while offering up a sacrifice of praise to God, that is, the fruit

Remembering that the **Gate** was at the east side of the tabernacle and we thank God that we can enter through the Gate because of His mercy, **Psalm 103:12** tell us that "As far as the **east** is from the west, so far hath he removed our transgressions from us." The gate separated the people from the Holy God, for God could only be approached with repentance and sacrifice, so as we enter we can thank God for removing our transgressions and allowing us to enter. Jesus referred to Himself as the gate or the door and anyone who enters through Jesus will receive eternal life (St. John 10:9). So we can enter in thanking God for Jesus who is the way, the truth and the life for no man comes to the Father in Heaven but by Him; we are looking unto Jesus who is the author and the finisher of our faith.

> *Refer to Photographs of Interest section beginning on page 119: The Gate Entrance (front view).*

The **Court** was a large, open-air of sacrifices, outside the limits of the Holy ground. The Brazen Altar and the Brazen Laver were in this area on the ground of the tabernacle and the Priest would enter into this area to offer up sacrifices with animal blood as atonement for their sin.

> *Refer to Photographs of Interest section beginning on page 119: The Court (right side view of the Tabernacle).*

The first two suggested Hebrew words for Praise are **Todah/Tawdah and Yadah**. The first two pieces of furniture in the tabernacle were the **Brazen Altar** and the **Brazen Laver**.

The Brazen Altar is located in the court where the blood was sprinkled on the four horns of the Altar, Exodus 27:1-8.

> *Refer to Photographs of Interest section beginning on page 119: The Brazen Altar.*

Symbolic Meaning: Atonement through Christ's sacrifice. (The reconciliation of man to God, the expiation of sin made by the obedience, personal suffering and death of Christ Jesus, as He made amends and suffered punishment for man's wrongdoings.)

Brazen Altar – is where we should thank God for receiving atonement through the sacrifice Jesus made at Calvary. We are recognizing the fact that we could not atone for our own sins and only the Blood of Jesus was proficient and capable of clearing us of all the charges of sin. We should also visualize Jesus and His crucifixion, when the blood came out of His side; He paid the price and bought us back from the fall; that was caused by the first Adam. Jesus' blood purged and cleansed us of all unrighteousness. Jesus became the propitiation for our sins, saying we deserve to die, but that He would take the punishment for us; therefore we should say thanks. The Father loved us so much, that even when we deserved to die, He sent His only Son in our place as a propitiation for us and the world (Romans 3:25; I John 2:2; I John 4:10).

There was a contract on our lives, but by the Blood of Jesus the contract was paid in full and He brought us back from the power of sin and death. Since we have been redeemed from the curse of the law, we should speak out and Say: "Thank You for Saving Me, Thank you for redeeming me from the hand of the enemy (Psalms 107:2). According to the riches of His grace, we have been redeemed through His blood and forgiven of our sins (Ephesians 1:7). Thank you Jesus, for redeeming us to God by your Blood (Revelations 5:9).

The next piece of furniture we will arrive at is the **Brazen Laver**.

Brazen Laver – is where the priest in the biblical days would come for cleansing, because they must be pure to enter into the presence of God. This furniture was a large bronze vessel placed in the court of the Jewish tabernacle where the officiating priests washed their hands and feet.

> *Refer to Photographs of Interest section beginning on page 119: The Brazen Laver.*

Symbolic Meaning: Spiritual renewal/regeneration by the Holy Spirit who is the Living Water of Life.

Brazen Laver – is now where we can be spiritually renewed by the Holy Spirit and receive spiritual regeneration. This is where we should thank God for the cleansing that Jesus provided for all the impurities that sin causes; because the wages of sin is death, but the gift of God is eternal life. According to the mercies of God we are saved by the washing of regeneration and renewing of the Holy Ghost, so we can continue on into the presence, thanking God that our sins are washed away. Jesus made reconciliation on our behalf, then, spiritually renewed us (Titus 3:5). As we picture the Laver Basin, we should shout thanks to Jesus for His Blood that washed and regenerated us, for His Word and for the water that came out of His side to wash us whiter than snow.

As we **YADAH** praises, we are remembering that Christ's sacrifice cleared us of all charges of sin, then purged us, cleansed us and made settle the score on our behalf.

I am reminded of Second Chronicles 20:19-21, where Jehoshaphat led the people of Judah into victory because the Lord gave Jehoshaphat's military success. A huge army was attacking them from the other side of the Dead Sea, but Jehoshaphat sought the Lord's advice. The Lord gave them instructions and told them not to be afraid because He would fight the battle. Furthermore, just to march down before their warriors and against the enemy with praise in their mouths and worship in their hearts, because He would set an ambush for the enemy. All Jehoshaphat and the army had to do was appoint musicians to play before the Lord, praising his majestic splendor and giving thanks to the Lord for His loyal love that endures.

The Levites obeyed and stood up to praise God with a loud noise; appointed singers and went out before the army. When they began to shout praises to the Lord, the Lord launched a sudden attack on the enemies, and the enemies turned on each other; they were all annihilated and Jehoshaphat and the army were able to gather spoils that were left by the enemies for three days.

Suggested Hebrew words of Praise and Worship when entering into God's Presence

Todah means to lift and extend your hands in a cup-like manner, as if you are offering up a sacrifice; but at the same time offering up thanks with the fruit of your lips, giving thanks continually.

In the biblical days the priests would come for cleansing before they entered into the Holy Place and would extend their hands in submission, because they were carrying an animal sacrifice. We do not sacrifice animals anymore, so we will just cup our hands in submission for God to accept or reject our praise. The word of God in **Psalms 50:23** lets us know that "Whoso offereth praise glorifieth me: and to him that ordereth his conversation aright will I shew the salvation of God." So, as we present our worship and praise toward God for acceptance or rejection, as an act of worship and devotion, commanding and regulating our sentiments toward God in an oral or verbal exchange, He will manifest His saving power.

As we enter into the presence of God, with a **YADAH** praise we should lift and extend our hands, throwing them out in front of us as if we are pressing into the presence of God. Remember Matthew 11:12, "From the days of John the Baptist until now the kingdom of heaven has suffered violence, and powerful and persuaded people lay hold of it." The Kingdom of God has been forcefully advancing since the days of John the Baptist, but because the flesh does not want to be in the Presence of God, we must render it powerless by compelling it to go into God's presence; so it can be cleaned more and more each time. We must enter into His presence with no reservation.

When we praise God and allow His praises to be in the assembly of His saints, the Lord will take delight in His people. He will save those who are not proud and make us feel like Kings. As we let the high praises of God be in our mouths and the Word in our hearts, God will execute vengeance upon the heathen, bind their kings with chains, and their nobles with fetters of iron.

As we express **YADAH**, we are recognizing the Atonement of Christ through His sacrifice. Atonement is to clear us of all charges of sin, then purge and cleanse us and make reconciliation on our behalf. We are also expressing YADAH because of our Spiritual Renewal and Regeneration by the Holy Spirit.

In II Chronicles 20:19-21 (The story of Jehoshaphat) the Levites stood up to praise God with a loud noise; appointed singers, and went out before the army. Just by them being obedient and giving thanks unto the Lord for his loyal love that endures; the Lord launched a sudden attack on the enemy which annihilated them. Jehoshaphat and His people were able to gather the spoils of the enemy for three days.

Yadah means lifting and extending your hands with all your strength, throwing them out as if you were stoning the enemy, expressing disapproval of Satan, who is the thief.

When we enter into God's presence, we are praising God with all of our heart, soul and strength and with confidence that we have a blood bought right to enter. Remembering, we have the authority over the enemy and he is subject to us. Then, we are going to take back everything that the enemy has stolen from us. As we throw out our hand as if we are stoning the enemy, we will joyfully take back our joy, peace, romance, finances etc., or whatever the enemy has stolen from us, with our weapon of praise. Since we have found out who the real thief is, he must pay (Proverbs 6:30-31).

Psalms 150 says, "Let high praise be in our mouth and a two edge sword in our hand, binding the power of the evil one with shackles and carrying out the defeated foes sentence."

We press into the presence of God with a posture of stoning the enemy and expressing displeasure in him for stealing our joy, peace, finances, romances, etc. We press in, with an assurance that everything the enemy has stolen will be returned. The Word of God promises, once a thief is caught, he must pay back seven times as much as he has stolen; even if it means selling everything in his house to pay it back (Proverbs 6:31). The enemy, who is the thief, will try to discourage us from entering into the Presence of God, so, we stone him with our praise. We also press into the presence of God with boldness, letting High Praise be in our mouths and a double-edged sword in our hand, which is The Word of God.

As we continue to picture ourselves entering into the presence of God, and through the replica of the heavens, we must tunnel our vision on Jesus and the work He did at Calvary. We must shut out everything else so we can boldly and successfully enter God's presence. Also, with the word of God in our mouths and heart, binding the power of the evil one with shackles and carrying out the defeated foes sentence with spiritual triumphant praise.

Holy Place

The next pieces of furniture in the tabernacle are the Table of Shewbread, Candlestand and Altar of Incense. The suggested Hebrew words of praise are: Halal, Shabach and Zamar.

> *Refer to Photographs of Interest section beginning on page 119: Table of Shewbread, Candlestand/ Golden Lampstand and Altar of Incense..*

Symbolic Meanings:

1. **Table of Shewbread** – Spiritual sustenance/ nourishment; Christ the Bread of Life

    (Present on the table were the twelve loaves of bread which represented the twelve tribes of Israel);

2. **Candlestand** – Spiritual illumination of Christ who is the Light of the World

    (The Lamp-stand was hammered from a single plate of pure gold and stood in the Holy Place on the south side, opposite the table of showbread. This lamp-stand held seven lamps, flat bowls in which a wick lay with one end in the oil of the bowl and the lit end hanging out. The idea conveyed that God's church is set to be a light giver in the world – Matthew 5:14, 16- Luke 12:35 and Phil. 2:15); and

3. **Altar of Incense** – Prayers of the saints which are acceptable supplication in the name of Jesus – Revelation 5:8

    (On the altar was a sweet smelling aroma of spices continually burning with fire taken from the Brazen Altar – the burning of the incense was a type of continual prayer).

Suggested Hebrew Words of Praise

Halal comes from the word Hallelujah which means to boast, rave, to celebrate to show forth adoration. It also means to act clamorously foolish or literally crazy about our God. It means for one to act undignified, shout out to God, scream, cry out and dance with all of your might as the Psalmist David did in II Samuel 6:14.

> *II Samuel 6:21-22 NKJV*
>
> *21 So David said to Michal, "It was before the LORD, who chose me instead of your father and all his house, to appoint me ruler over the people of the LORD, over Israel. Therefore I will play music before the LORD.*
>
> *22 And I will be even more **undignified than this**, and will be humble in my own sight. But as for the maidservants of whom you have spoken, by them I will be held in honor."*
>
> *Shabach (Psalms 47:1) Psalm 47*
>
> *¹ clap your hands, all ye people; shout unto God with the voice of triumph.*

Shabach is praise with a loud voice of expression and a loud expression clapping our hands and shouting unto God with a voice of triumph. It is proclaiming with a loud voice His majestic power, against any walls in our lives, such as: depression, oppression etc. or spiritual barriers that will keep us from getting our abundant victory. As we enter in the presence with a loud expression we are to clap our hands, which comes from the Greek word "Tahkah" meaning to clatter, clang, described as the blowing of a trumpet and sounding the alarm. This entire expression indicates energy and enthusiasm. One should and will imagine Satan between your hands of authority and we are crushing his kingdom down. Also, since we are the Royal Priesthood or the Kings, we can just clap our hands and our servants will come to our aid. At this time of praise and worship we can dispatch our angels to go and cause whatever we have asked in Jesus' name to come to pass or manifest. For we must remember that we do have ministering spirits that serve us (Hebrews 1:14) and we have angels that have charge over us (Psalm 91:11); which provides safekeeping over everything concerning us. So, we enter into God's presence proclaiming our victory and authority over everything that tries to hinder our entrance.

> *Zamar (Psalms 150:1-6)*
>
> ¹ *Praise ye the LORD. Praise God in his sanctuary: praise him in the firmament of his power.*
>
> ² *Praise him for his mighty acts: praise him according to his excellent greatness.*
>
> ³ *Praise him with the sound of the trumpet: praise him with the psaltery and harp.*
>
> ⁴ *Praise him with the timbrel and dance: praise him with stringed instruments and organs.*
>
> ⁵ *Praise him upon the loud cymbals: praise him upon the high sounding cymbals.*
>
> ⁶ *Let every thing that hath breath praise the LORD. Praise ye the LORD.*

Zamar is a Hebrew Praise word that means to praise God by touching the strings of an instrument, accompanied by our voices, celebrating in song and psalms. Also, it means allowing our voices to be an instrument in God's hand that He might pluck the strings of our vocal cords, with Psalms, Hymns and Spiritual songs, letting our heart make the music.

As we continue to enter into the Presence of God, thanking Him and envisioning Heaven, we must visualize each piece of furniture and recognize that it represents the plan for our Salvation. Each piece of the Tabernacle Furniture depicts the redemptive work of Jesus Christ.

Hebrews 8:5

5 Who serve unto the example and shadow of heavenly things, as Moses was admonished of God when he was about to make the tabernacle: for, See, saith he, that thou make all things according to the pattern shewed to thee in the mount.

Exodus 25:40

40 And look that thou make them after their pattern, which was shewed thee in the mount.

Table of Shewbread: Represents Spiritual Sustenance – Jesus said in St. John 6:51 "I am the living bread that came down from heaven. If anyone eats from this bread he will live forever. The bread that I will give for the life of the world is my flesh." The loaves of bread, which the priest of the week placed before the Lord on the golden table in the sanctuary, represented the twelve tribes of Israel. In the Holy Place, this bread was made of fine flour unleavened, and was changed every Sabbath. This bread was to be eaten by the priests only.

Table of Showbread – This is where we give thanks to Jesus Christ for giving us life and for being our nourishment. He is the Living Bread. Jesus said in St. John 6:48 "I am the bread of life." The table served as a symbol of God as the provider of the food for life. He is our provision and sustenance. He is the supplier. The loaves were consecrated to the Lord and used at the Love Feast and the Lord's Table. So, as we imagine the showbread table, we can thank Jesus for revealing Himself as the bread of Life; for He is the Beasty One who nourishes and supplies. Also, we can thank Jesus for sending the Holy Spirit to quench our thirst with the Water of Life to never thirst again.

Candlestand – Spiritual Illumination – Christ the Light of the World and especially of His own people – a gold Lampstand stood in the Holy Place, opposite the table of showbread. It held seven lamps, flat bowls in which a wick lay with one end in the oil of the bowl and the lighted end hanging out. St. John 8:12 "I am the light of the world."

The **Candlestand** or Lampstand served as a symbol of God, being the light that guided for the children of Israel during the mass departure from Egypt. This represented that God has and will lead us out of darkness into His marvelous light. However, it was a type of Christ, who is our light. The oil that was burned in the lamps was a symbol of the Holy Spirit. We must be reminded that Olives were beaten and crushed in order to obtain the oil, extracted from the pulp; and Jesus was beaten for us so we could be healed and receive the anointing of the Holy Spirit. The closer we get to the Holy of Holies, the more valuable the materials get. If we notice, the furniture went from bronze to gold; which marks a more pure worth. The further we move into the tabernacle the closer we are getting to the presence of the Most High God. Therefore, we should visualize the Candlestand

and thank Jesus for being a light in darkness and the light unto our pathway and a lamp unto our feet.

The tabernacle was a symbol of the Old Testament system when approaching God. The High Priest was allowed to enter once a year for the sins of the people; however, as long as the tabernacle was yet standing, the way into the Holy Place was concealed or hidden. When Jesus cried out with a loud voice on the cross and breathed his last breath; the curtain separating the Holy of Holies from the Holy Place and was torn in two from top to bottom. This symbolized that we now have access to God and can boldly enter into His presence. We no longer need a man to intervene for us or to bring sacrifices for our sins to God. Through Christ and faith in Him, we may approach God with freedom and confidence; for Jesus was the Last Lamb that was slain.

Therefore, we can go boldly go into the holiest by the Blood of Jesus, who is our Salvation, because He has consecrated us through the veil. Jesus opened the way through the curtain into the inner sanctuary by the sacrifice of His flesh. Just as the curtain was split, so Christ's body was broken for us to give us access into God's presence.

The Holy Spirit signifies the way into the Holy of Holies and I Corinthians 6:19 lets us now know that our bodies are the temple of the Holy Ghost which is in us, and we do not belong to ourselves but to our God. Jesus Christ who is now our High Priest comes by a greater and more perfect tabernacle which is not made with hands. Jesus entered once into the holy place by his own blood and obtained eternal redemption for all of us (Hebrews 9:11-12).

Holy of Holies

As we enter into the second veil which is the Holy of Holies, the furniture is the Ark of the Covenant, the Mercy Seat and the Very Presence of God (Shekinah). The suggested Hebrew words of praise are **Barak** and **Tehillah**.

Barak means to bow down before our Maker and to kneel in reverence to our King, Lord and Majesty. Psalms 95:6 instructs us to bow down; falling on our knees in a posture of worship; to kneel before the Lord our Maker and love Him. Barak in the Hebrew means to rock back and forth, flowing as the wind of the Spirit of God blows soft and easy upon us. I believe at this point, we are so close, where we can feel the very breath of God, breathing into us the Breath of life. We are yielding in total consent, as we say: "Breathe into me Oh Lord the Breath of Life."

Tehillah means to sing in the Spirit, conveying love messages to God and thanking Him for a new impartation. I believe in this area and position of the tabernacle, we are strictly worshipping; but not in the dance. At this stage of worship we should become still and prepare for intimacy. We cannot become intimate, close and personal while we are praising clamorously. At this stage of worship we should not being express to others, how good God is, but only express our love toward Jesus Christ. Intimacy is a private and dear time to become pregnant with the things of God, in order to birth these things into His Kingdom here on earth. We want to value each second in God's presence.

Mercy Seat and Shekinah

The Very Presence: Christ as "Mercy Seat" Life of God and Shekinah-Holy Spirit as the imparted Life of God.

Mercy Seat and the Very Presence of God is a symbol of God's throne protected by Cherubim's. The Cherubim's are angelic beings associated with guarding and bearing God's throne. They were associated with the worship of God Almighty. The High Priest would sprinkle blood on and in front of the Mercy Seat in the shape of a cross, and the atonement was made by God for His people. So now, since we have been chosen to be the Royal Priesthood, we must sprinkle our genuine Worship at the Mercy Seat, as an example of thanks and love for Calvary and what we obtain because of the Cross. We should reverence God for sending His only Son to shed His Blood, so that we might have the right to the Tree of Life. At this stage of the Tabernacle, we are in awe, realizing it was of the Lord's mercies that we were not consumed, because His compassion did not fail. We should be appreciative and overjoyed that His mercies and compassion are rendered to us new every morning and that God's faithfulness is great! (Lamentations 3:22-23)

HOLY OF HOLIES suggested Hebrew word: TEHILLAH –

Psalms 22:3

God inhabits the praises of His people;

St John 4:20-24

The Father seeketh such to worship His in Spirit and in Truth;

Luke 1:34 & 35; 42

The power of the Highest will hover over you; overshadow you like a shining cloud.

We are actually in the presence of God, at His Mercy Seat, and the Glory of God is saturating and consuming us with His Power. The Glory of God has enveloped us in His Glory, endured us with His Power and endowed us with His Anointing. In His Presences is the Fullness of Joy and at His Right Hand are pleasures forever more.

Instructions for Demonstration:

Assume our positions and posture of praise and worship and that is with the lifting of our Holy hands in the sanctuary and blessing His name with the fruit of our lips.

Begin to thank Jesus that He is our God and let us proceed to enter into the presence of our King.

Let us now actually invoke the presence of God into our situation or circumstance. For even at home, we can invoke the presence of God into our condition or events. Let us now exercise these instructions applying them to the need.

1. Tunnel your vision upon God and have an encounter with Heaven, by remembering the sacrifice at Calvary.

2. Shut out everyone else and see Jesus bigger that your circumstance, magnify Him.

3. Yield yourself in worship, so that the power of the Highest will overshadow you as He did Mary in the book of Luke 1:35.

"And the angel answered and said unto her, The Holy Ghost shall come upon thee, and the power of the Highest shall overshadow thee: therefore also that holy thing which shall be born of thee shall be called the Son of God."

4. Forgetting not your benefits but thanking God for them (Psalms 103:1-5), for He forgave us our iniquities, heals all our disease, redeemed our lives from destruction, crowns us with loving kindness and tender mercies, satisfies our mouths with good things, so our youth is renewed like the eagles.

5. Remember, Psalms 115:17 says "The dead go in silence and praise not the Lord."

6. So, Bless our God ye people and make the voice of His praise be heard (Psalms 66: 8-9).

As we are entering into God Holy of Holies, we must keep in mind that if it had not been for Jesus' blood, we would not have the right to the tree of life. If it had not been for the blood of Jesus, we would not be able to enter into the presence of God boldly. Jesus' blood has given us life and saved us from eternal damnation. His blood also made reparation for our sin and caused reconciliation between God and man, plus, blotted out all of our sins. Jesus' Blood redeemed us and the contract that was on our lives was paid in full at Calvary and the hold of sin and death was broken. We were justified by the Blood of Jesus as if we never sinned and His blood acquitted us of guilt. We were sanctified by is blood and set apart and for the remission of our sins, Jesus paid the debt and then cancelled it. His blood gave us overcoming power and delivered us from the power of darkness and translated us into the kingdom. We have been set free from the captivity of sin and where the spirit of the Lord is, there is liberty (II Cor. 3:17). Most of all, we have been forgiven and pardoned of sin, Psalms 103:12 says "As far as the east is from the west, so far hath he removed our transgressions from us."

The next pieces of furniture in the tabernacle are:

> *Refer to Photographs of Interest section beginning on page 119: The Ark of the Covenant.*

The Ark was most sacred of all. Here, the Hebrews kept a copy of the Ten Commandments which summarized the whole Covenant. The covenant relationship created by Christ, gives us access to God and through Christ we are able to receive every promise given. The Ark was the symbol of God's presence, and the place where He would meet and speak with Moses. Through this covenant, God gives us access to all of His promises. Christ, as the covenant, is confirmation of our relationship in order to get access to God. So, in our covenant relationship with God we are able to put on Christ and enter into God's presence boldly.

James 4:8 comforts us in knowing that if we draw nigh to God He will draw nigh to us; for He has clothed us with the Garments of Salvation and covered us with the Robe of Righteousness. Therefore, when God see us He sees the Blood and Righteousness; for II Corinthians 5:21 reassures us that God sent Christ, who never sinned, to be the offering for our sin, so that we might become the Righteousness of God in Him.

As a bridegroom decks himself with ornaments and as a bride adorns herself with her jewels, we must garnish ourselves with Worship; presenting acceptable and genuine reverence to our Lord and Savior. Therefore, as we envision the Ark, we are thanking Jesus that through His Blood He provided all of His promises through a covenant relationship with Him.

> *Refer to Photographs of Interest section beginning on page 119: Golden Urn, containing the manna, Aaron's Rod and the Stone tablets of the Covenant.*

In this Ark was the Golden Urn containing the Manna, Aaron's rod that budded, and the Stone Tablets of the Covenant (Hebrews 9:4).

- **The Manna** – was referred to by our Lord as "bread from heaven" and was a symbol of Him. Apostle Paul in I Corinthians 10:3 refers to the manna as "spiritual food;"

- **Aaron's Rod** – was kept in the Holy of Holies; inside of the Ark, as a token of the divine will of God and miracles – the Rod had budded, blossomed and borne fruit, which is an example of: "the three stages of vegetable life made visible;"

- **The Covenant Tablets of Stone** – was written by the very finger of God (Exodus 31:18), to express the demonstration of the Power and Authority of God; and the words of the covenant was "The Ten Commandments" which attest of the Divine Will or the Covenant;

- **The Lid of the Ark** – was a solid plate of gold; it was that whereon the blood of the yearly atonement was sprinkled by the High Priest. Derived from the notion of its

Symbolic Meanings: The Divine Presence of God – Access to God through the Covenant and Christ as the covenant grounds to a relationship. The provision of Christ's Blood bought us the right to enter into God's Presence. The mercy of God through Christ Jesus has imparted the Life of God in us. The Presence and the divine Glory of God will manifest upon us; therefore, we are allowed to enter into God's presence, thanking Jesus for praying and interceding on our behalf.

> *Refer to Photographs of Interest section beginning on page 119: The Ark and the Mercy Seat.*

Now, imagine and tunnel your vision on the Mercy Seat and the Shekinah Glory of God; which is His Very Presence as we enter into our encounter with God.

Mark 15:38

38 And the veil of the temple was rent in twain from the top to the bottom.

Hebrews 9:8

8 The Holy Ghost this signifying, that the way into the holiest of all was not yet made manifest, while as the first tabernacle was yet standing:

Hebrews 10:19-20

19 Having therefore, brethren, boldness to enter into the holiest by the blood of Jesus,

20 By a new and living way, which he hath consecrated for us, through the veil, that is to say, his flesh;

In God's presence we have the fullness of Joy and at His right hand are pleasures forevermore. The saints of God can expect an encounter or a mountain top experience.

Some things to expect at your encounter or mountain top experience:

1. Intimacy with your Celestial Body which is the heavenly body and is the part of us that is the New Creation, not your Terrestrial Body which pertains to our earth suit and the flesh;

2. Quality time and conversation for your purpose and call;

3. God reveals our son-ship and/or new relationship;

4. Receiving divine secrets;

5. God opens our minds to view our pleasures forevermore;

6. We gain strength and joy;

7. Strategies for our purpose is delivered to us; and

8. God renews us by transforming, purifying, re-educating and re-directing us for continual work after we return from our mountain top experience.

Test Questions

Name _____

Praise and Worship Test Score _____

Please Fill in the Blank with the Correct Answer.

1. A praise gathering is a _____ of God's might, power and purpose.

2. Praise is a response acknowledging God's _____ and _____.

3. Worship means to ascribe _____ to God.

4. Worship is the response acknowledging God's presence of:

   a. _____

   b. _____

   c. _____

5. When God inhabits our praise, He brings all of His attributes with Him and eight of His attributes are as follow:

   - Jehovah Jireh - He brings _____ and _____.

   - Jehovah - Rophe - He brings _____ and _____.

   - Jehovah - Tsidkenu - He brings His righteousness from _____.

   - Jehovah - M'Kaddesh - He brings _____ from sin.

- Jehovah - Shalom - He brings _____ for our Spirit Man.
- Jehovah - Shammah - He is always _____ to bring peace.
- Jehovah - Nissi - He is our banner, _____ and _____.
- Jehovah - Rohi - He is our protection and _____.

6. One Greek Word for Worship is Proskueno, Pros means _____ and Kueno means to _____.

7. No Flesh should _____ in the presence of God.

8. The flesh is the Natural _____ and not the _____ Man.

9. The flesh is our will, our _____, our _____ component with the lust and the _____ of the body.

10. Roman 3:20 says: "There shall no _____ be justified in His sight."

11. II Timothy 3:16-17 says: All Scripture is given by inspiration of God and is profitable for _____, for _____, for _____, for _____ in righteousness, that the man of God may be perfect thoroughly furnished unto all good works.

12. Pneuma denotes "the wind," the _____ refers to the Spirit.

13. Ruah means to _____, air strength, wind (present direction), breeze, spirit courage, temper, spirit.

14. When the Redeemed Man allows his breath to blow, to release the vapor from the _____, his breath invisibly Formulates a _____ quality of air that actually builds an invisible _____ for God to _____.

15. When entering into the presence of God there are seven levels of praise and they are:

    - **Todah-Tawdah** the lifting and extending your hands in a _____ manner.

    - **Yadah** - Lifting and extending your hands, with all of your strength, _____ them out as if you are _____ the enemy.

    - **Halal** - (Hallelujah), means clamorously Foolish, to _____, to _____, to _____, to show forth adoration and admiration toward God.

    - **Shabach** - _____ voice of expression or a loud expression of clapping of your hands.

    - **Zamar** - to touch the _____.

    - **Barak** - to bow down before your _____.

    - **Tehillah** - to sing in the _____ conveying love messages to God.

16. Keep your spiritual vision tunneled toward the face of God. Seeking His face and not His hand. Each step, we must remember to thank God with the fruits of our lips and:

    - Visualizing the _____ and praising God that Jesus was the last Lamb to be slain for our sins.

- Visualizing the _____ and thanking Jesus that his blood washed all our sins away.

- Visualizing the _____ and thanking Jesus for revealing Himself as the Bread of Life.

- Visualizing the _____, and thanking Christ for being the Light of the World.

- Visualizing the _____ and thanking Jesus for sitting at the right hand of the Father praying for us and interceding on our behalf.

- Visualizing the _____ and thanking Jesus for providing all His promises through a covenant relationship.

- Visualizing the _____ and the _____ (Shekinah Glory); and thanking Jesus for allowing us to be in His presence.

Answers to Test Questions

1. Celebration
2. Deeds;
   Mighty Acts
3. Worth
4. a. Lordship;
   b. Kingship;
   c. Majesty
5. Provision, Success;
   Healing, Soundness;
   Sin;
   Sanctification;
   Peace;
   There;
   Protection, Victory;
   Security
6. Toward;
   Kiss
7. Glory
8. Man, Spiritual
9. Emotions, personality, craving
10. Flesh
11. Doctrine, Reproof, Correction, Instructions
12. Breath
13. Breathe (life of the man)
14. Inner Man, Fleeting, Throne, Inhabit

15. Cup-like;
    Throwing, Stoning:
    Boast, Rave, Celebrate;
    Loud;
    Strings;
    Maker;
    Spirit

16. Brazen Alter;
    Brazen Laver;
    Table of Shewbread;
    Candle-stand;
    Altar of Incense;
    Ark of the Covenant;
    Mercy Seat, Presence of God

Now We are Embraced in His Love – Enveloped in His Glory and Endued with His Power

Other Scriptures to refer to as you proof the text of the information given:

Psalm 33:1

[1] Rejoice in the LORD, O ye righteous: for praise is comely for the upright.

Proverbs 4:7

[7] Wisdom is the principal thing; therefore get wisdom: and with all thy getting get understanding.

1 Peter 3:15

[15] But sanctify the Lord God in your hearts: and be ready always to give an answer to every man that asketh you a reason of the hope that is in you with meekness and fear:

Psalm 115:17-18

[17] The dead praise not the LORD, neither any that go down into silence.

[18] But we will bless the LORD from this time forth and for evermore. Praise the LORD.

Isaiah 38:18

[18] For the grave cannot praise thee, death can not celebrate thee: they that go down into the pit cannot hope for thy truth.

Luke 10:27

[27] And he answering said, Thou shalt love the Lord thy God with all thy heart, and with all thy soul, and with all thy strength,

and with all thy mind; and thy neighbour as thyself.

Psalm 148:1-14

[1] Praise ye the LORD. Praise ye the LORD from the heavens: praise him in the heights.

[2] Praise ye him, all his angels: praise ye him, all his hosts.

[3] Praise ye him, sun and moon: praise him, all ye stars of light.

[4] Praise him, ye heavens of heavens, and ye waters that be above the heavens.

[5] Let them praise the name of the LORD: for he commanded, and they were created.

[6] He hath also stablished them for ever and ever: he hath made a decree which shall not pass.

[7] Praise the LORD from the earth, ye dragons, and all deeps:

[8] Fire, and hail; snow, and vapours; stormy wind fulfilling his word:

[9] Mountains, and all hills; fruitful trees, and all cedars:

[10] Beasts, and all cattle; creeping things, and flying fowl:

[11] Kings of the earth, and all people; princes, and all judges of the earth:

[12] Both young men, and maidens; old men, and children:

[13] Let them praise the name of the LORD: for his name alone is excellent; his glory is above the earth and heaven.

¹⁴ He also exalteth the horn of his people, the praise of all his saints; even of the children of Israel, a people near unto him. Praise ye the LORD.

2 Samuel 6:14-23

¹⁴ And David danced before the LORD with all his might; and David was girded with a linen ephod.

¹⁵ So David and all the house of Israel brought up the ark of the LORD with shouting, and with the sound of the trumpet.

¹⁶ And as the ark of the LORD came into the city of David, Michal Saul's daughter looked through a window, and saw King David leaping and dancing before the LORD; and she despised him in her heart.

¹⁷ And they brought in the ark of the LORD, and set it in his place, in the midst of the tabernacle that David had pitched for it: and David offered burnt offerings and peace offerings before the LORD.

¹⁸ And as soon as David had made an end of offering burnt offerings and peace offerings, he blessed the people in the name of the LORD of hosts.

¹⁹ And he dealt among all the people, even among the whole multitude of Israel, as well to the women as men, to every one a cake of bread, and a good piece of flesh, and a flagon of wine. So all the people departed every one to his house.

²⁰ Then David returned to bless his household. And Michal the daughter of Saul came out to meet David, and said, How glorious was the king of Israel to day, who uncovered himself to day in the eyes of the handmaids of his servants, as one of the vain fellows shamelessly uncovereth himself!

21 And David said unto Michal, It was before the LORD, which chose me before thy father, and before all his house, to appoint me ruler over the people of the LORD, over Israel: therefore will I play before the LORD.

22 And I will yet be more vile than thus, and will be base in mine own sight: and of the maidservants which thou hast spoken of, of them shall I be had in honour.

23 Therefore Michal the daughter of Saul had no child unto the day of her death.

Psalm 100:1-2

1 Make a joyful noise unto the LORD, all ye lands.

2 Serve the LORD with gladness: come before his presence with singing.

Psalm 95:2

2 Let us come before his presence with thanksgiving, and make a joyful noise unto him with psalms.

1 Peter 2:9

9 But ye are a chosen generation, a royal priesthood, an holy nation, a peculiar people; that ye should shew forth the praises of him who hath called you out of darkness into his marvellous light;

Psalm 149:1

¹ Praise ye the LORD. Sing unto the LORD a new song, and his praise in the congregation of saints.

Isaiah 61:3

³ To appoint unto them that mourn in Zion, to give unto them beauty for ashes, the oil of joy for mourning, the garment of praise for the spirit of heaviness; that they might be called trees of righteousness, the planting of the LORD, that he might be glorified.

Psalm 134:2 (KJV)

² Lift up your hands in the sanctuary, and bless the LORD

Psalm 63:4 (KJV)

⁴ Thus will I bless thee while I live: I will lift up my hands in thy name

Psalm 47:1 (KJV)

¹ clap your hands, all ye people; shout unto God with the voice of triumph.

Psalm 24:7 (KJV)

⁷ Lift up your heads, O ye gates; and be ye lift up, ye everlasting doors; and the King of glory shall come in.

Psalm 24:9 (KJV)

⁹ Lift up your heads, O ye gates; even lift them up, ye everlasting doors; and the King of glory shall come in.

Psalm 138:2 (KJV)

² I will worship toward thy holy temple, and praise thy name for thy loving kindness and for thy truth: for thou hast magnified thy word above all thy name.

Psalm 66:8 (KJV)

⁸ bless our God, ye people, and make the voice of his praise to be heard:

Psalm 98:4-5 (KJV)

⁴ Make a joyful noise unto the LORD, all the earth: make a loud noise, and rejoice, and sing praise.

⁵ Sing unto the LORD with the harp; with the harp, and the voice of a psalm.

Psalm 63:3 (KJV)

³ Because thy loving kindness is better than life, my lips shall praise thee.

Psalm 71:23-24 (KJV)

²³ My lips shall greatly rejoice when I sing unto thee; and my soul, which thou hast redeemed.

²⁴ My tongue also shall talk of thy righteousness all the day long: for they are confounded, for they are brought unto shame, that seek my hurt.

Psalm 104:34 (KJV)

³⁴ My meditation of him shall be sweet: I will be glad in the LORD.

Psalm 6:5 (KJV)

⁵ For in death there is no remembrance of thee: in the grave who shall give thee thanks?

Psalm 145:21 (KJV)

²¹ My mouth shall speak the praise of the LORD: and let all flesh bless his holy name for ever and ever.

Psalm 149:3 (KJV)

³ Let them praise his name in the dance: let them sing praises unto him with the timbrel and harp.

Psalm 150:4 (KJV)

⁴ Praise him with the timbrel and dance: praise him with stringed instruments and organs.

Psalm 28:7 (KJV)

⁷ The LORD is my strength and my shield; my heart trusted in him, and I am helped: therefore my heart greatly rejoiceth; and with my song will I praise him.

Psalm 86:2 (KJV)

² Preserve my soul; for I am holy: O thou my God, save thy servant that trusteth in thee.

Psalm 108:1 (KJV)

¹ God, my heart is fixed; I will sing and give praise, even with my glory.

Psalm 9:1 (KJV)

¹ I will praise thee, O LORD, with my whole heart; I will shew forth all thy marvellous works.

Psalm 111:1 (KJV)

¹ Praise ye the LORD. I will praise the LORD with my whole heart, in the assembly of the upright, and in the congregation.

Judges 5:9 (KJV)

⁹ My heart is toward the governors of Israel, that offered themselves willingly among the people. Bless ye the LORD.

Psalm 150:3-4 (KJV)

³ Praise him with the sound of the trumpet: praise him with the psaltery and harp.

⁴ Praise him with the timbrel and dance: praise him with stringed instruments and organs.

1 Chronicles 23:5 (KJV)

⁵ Moreover four thousand were porters; and four thousand praised the LORD with the instruments which I made, said David, to praise therewith.

Psalm 33:2 (KJV)

² Praise the LORD with harp: sing unto him with the psaltery and an instrument of ten strings.

Psalm 149:3 (KJV)

³ Let them praise his name in the dance: let them sing praises unto him with the timbrel and harp.

2 Chronicles 5:13 (KJV)

¹³ It came even to pass, as the trumpeters and singers were as one, to make one sound to be heard in praising and thanking the LORD; and when they lifted up their voice with the trumpets and cymbals and instruments of musick, and praised the LORD, saying, For he is good; for his mercy endureth for ever: that then the house was filled with a cloud, even the house of the LORD;

Psalm 147:7(KJV)

⁷ Sing unto the LORD with thanksgiving; sing praise upon the harp unto our God:

2 Chronicles 30:21 (KJV)

²¹ And the children of Israel that were present at Jerusalem kept the feast of unleavened bread seven days with great gladness: and the Levites and the priests praised the LORD day by day, singing with loud instruments unto the LORD.

Psalm 144:9 (KJV)

⁹ I will sing a new song unto thee, O God: upon a psaltery and an instrument of ten strings will I sing praises unto thee.

2 Chronicles 7:6 (KJV)

⁶ And the priests waited on their offices: the Levites also with instruments of musick of the LORD, which David the king had made to praise the LORD, because his mercy endureth for ever, when David praised by their ministry; and the priests sounded trumpets before them, and all Israel stood.

Psalm 71:22 (KJV)

²² I will also praise thee with the psaltery, even thy truth, O my God: unto thee will I sing with the harp, O thou Holy One of Israel.

Isaiah 38:20 (KJV)

²⁰ The LORD was ready to save me: therefore we will sing my songs to the stringed instruments all the days of our life in the house of the LORD.

Isaiah 38:20 (KJV)

²⁰ The LORD was ready to save me: therefore we will sing my songs to the stringed instruments all the days of our life in the house of the LORD.

1 Chronicles 23:5 (KJV)

⁵ Moreover four thousand were porters; and four thousand praised the LORD with the instruments which I made, said David, to praise therewith.

Psalm 33:2 (KJV)

² Praise the LORD with harp: sing unto him with the psaltery and an instrument of ten strings.

Psalm 149:3 (KJV)

³ Let them praise his name in the dance: let them sing praises unto him with the timbrel and harp.

2 Chronicles 5:13(KJV)

¹³ It came even to pass, as the trumpeters and singers were as one, to make one sound to be heard in praising and thanking the LORD; and when they lifted up their voice with the trumpets and cymbals and instruments of musick, and praised the LORD, saying, For he is good; for his mercy endureth for ever: that then the house was filled with a cloud, even the house of the LORD;

Psalm 147:7 (KJV)

⁷ Sing unto the LORD with thanksgiving; sing praise upon the harp unto our God:

2 Chronicles 30:21 (KJV)

²¹ And the children of Israel that were present at Jerusalem kept the feast of unleavened bread seven days with great gladness: and the Levites and the priests

praised the LORD day by day, singing with loud instruments unto the LORD.

Psalm 144:9 (KJV)

⁹ I will sing a new song unto thee, O God: upon a psaltery and an instrument of ten strings will I sing praises unto thee.

2 Chronicles 7:6 (KJV)

⁶ And the priests waited on their offices: the Levites also with instruments of musick of the LORD, which David the king had made to praise the LORD, because his mercy endureth for ever, when David praised by their ministry; and the priests sounded trumpets before them, and all Israel stood

Psalm 71:22 (KJV)

²² I will also praise thee with the psaltery, even thy truth, O my God: unto thee will I sing with the harp, O thou Holy One of Israel.

Isaiah 38:20 (KJV)

²⁰ The LORD was ready to save me: therefore we will sing my songs to the stringed instruments all the days of our life in the house of the LORD.

2 Chronicles 29:27 (KJV)

²⁷ And Hezekiah commanded to offer the burnt offering upon the altar. And when the burnt offering began, the song of the LORD began also with the trumpets, and with the instruments ordained by David king of Israel.

John 14:17-18 (NIV)

¹⁷ *the Spirit of truth. The world cannot accept him, because it neither sees him nor knows him. But you know him, for he lives with you and will be in you.*

2 Corinthians 4:4 (KJV)

⁴ *In whom the god of this world hath blinded the minds of them which believe not, lest the light of the glorious gospel of Christ, who is the image of God, should shine unto them.*

I John 2:15-16 KJV

¹⁵ *Love not the world, neither the things that are in the world. If any man love the world, the love of the Father is not in him.*

¹⁶ *For all that is in the world, the lust of the flesh, and the lust of the eyes, and the pride of life, is not of the Father, but is of the world.*

Ephesians 3:20 (KJV)

²⁰ *Now unto him that is able to do exceeding abundantly above all that we ask or think, according to the power that worketh in us,*

Hebrews 8:5 (KJV)

⁵ *Who serve unto the example and shadow of heavenly things, as Moses was admonished of God when he was about to make the tabernacle: for, See, saith he, that thou make all things according to the pattern shewed to thee in the mount.*

Exodus 25:40 (KJV)

⁴⁰ *And look that thou make them after their pattern, which was shewed thee in the mount.*

Hebrews 9:11-28 (KJV)

¹¹ But Christ being come an high priest of good things to come, by a greater and more perfect tabernacle, not made with hands, that is to say, not of this building;

¹² Neither by the blood of goats and calves, but by his own blood he entered in once into the holy place, having obtained eternal redemption for us.

¹³ For if the blood of bulls and of goats, and the ashes of an heifer sprinkling the unclean, sanctifieth to the purifying of the flesh:

¹⁴ How much more shall the blood of Christ, who through the eternal Spirit offered himself without spot to God, purge your conscience from dead works to serve the living God?

¹⁵ And for this cause he is the mediator of the new testament, that by means of death, for the redemption of the transgressions that were under the first testament, they which are called might receive the promise of eternal inheritance.

¹⁶ For where a testament is, there must also of necessity be the death of the testator.

¹⁷ For a testament is of force after men are dead: otherwise it is of no strength at all while the testator liveth.

¹⁸ Whereupon neither the first testament was dedicated without blood.

¹⁹ For when Moses had spoken every precept to all the people according to the law, he took the blood of calves and of goats, with water, and scarlet wool, and hyssop, and sprinkled both the book, and all the people,

20 Saying, This is the blood of the testament which God hath enjoined unto you.

21 Moreover he sprinkled with blood both the tabernacle, and all the vessels of the ministry.

22 And almost all things are by the law purged with blood; and without shedding of blood is no remission.

23 It was therefore necessary that the patterns of things in the heavens should be purified with these; but the heavenly things themselves with better sacrifices than these.

24 For Christ is not entered into the holy places made with hands, which are the figures of the true; but into heaven itself, now to appear in the presence of God for us:

25 Nor yet that he should offer himself often, as the high priest entereth into the holy place every year with blood of others;

26 For then must he often have suffered since the foundation of the world: but now once in the end of the world hath he appeared to put away sin by the sacrifice of himself.

27 And as it is appointed unto men once to die, but after this the judgment:

28 So Christ was once offered to bear the sins of many; and unto them that look for him shall he appear the second time without sin unto salvation.

Hebrews 9:16-20 (KJV)

¹⁶ For where a testament is, there must also of necessity be the death of the testator.

¹⁷ For a testament is of force after men are dead: otherwise it is of no strength at all while the testator liveth.

¹⁸ Whereupon neither the first testament was dedicated without blood.

¹⁹ For when Moses had spoken every precept to all the people according to the law, he took the blood of calves and of goats, with water, and scarlet wool, and hyssop, and sprinkled both the book, and all the people,

²⁰ Saying, This is the blood of the testament which God hath enjoined unto you.

Matthew 26:28 (KJV)

²⁸ For this is my blood of the new testament, which is shed for many for the remission of sins.

Mark 14:24 (KJV)

²⁴ And he said unto them, This is my blood of the new testament, which is shed for many.

Hebrews 9: 1-28 KJV

¹ Then verily the first covenant had also ordinances of divine service, and a worldly sanctuary.

² For there was a tabernacle made; the first, wherein was the candlestick, and the table, and the shewbread; which is called the sanctuary.

³ And after the second veil, the tabernacle which is called the Holiest of all;

⁴ Which had the golden censer, and the ark of the covenant overlaid round about with gold, wherein was the golden pot that had manna, and Aaron's rod that budded, and the tables of the covenant;

⁵ And over it the cherubims of glory shadowing the mercyseat; of which we cannot now speak particularly.

⁶ Now when these things were thus ordained, the priests went always into the first tabernacle, accomplishing the service of God.

⁷ But into the second went the high priest alone once every year, not without blood, which he offered for himself, and for the errors of the people:

⁸ The Holy Ghost this signifying, that the way into the holiest of all was not yet made manifest, while as the first tabernacle was yet standing:

⁹ Which was a figure for the time then present, in which were offered both gifts and sacrifices, that could not make him that did the service perfect, as pertaining to the conscience;

¹⁰ Which stood only in meats and drinks, and divers washings, and carnal ordinances, imposed on them until the time of reformation.

¹¹ But Christ being come an high priest of good things to come, by a greater and more perfect tabernacle, not made with hands, that is to say, not of this building;

¹² Neither by the blood of goats and calves, but by his own blood he entered in once into the holy place, having obtained eternal redemption for us.

¹³ For if the blood of bulls and of goats, and the ashes of an heifer sprinkling the unclean, sanctifieth to the purifying of the flesh:

¹⁴ How much more shall the blood of Christ, who through the eternal Spirit offered himself without spot to God, purge your conscience from dead works to serve the living God?

¹⁵ And for this cause he is the mediator of the new testament, that by means of death, for the redemption of the transgressions that were under the first testament, they which are called might receive the promise of eternal inheritance.

¹⁶ For where a testament is, there must also of necessity be the death of the testator.

¹⁷ For a testament is of force after men are dead: otherwise it is of no strength at all while the testator liveth.

¹⁸ Whereupon neither the first testament was dedicated without blood.

¹⁹ For when Moses had spoken every precept to all the people according to the law, he took the blood of calves and of goats, with water, and scarlet wool, and hyssop, and sprinkled both the book, and all the people,

²⁰ Saying, This is the blood of the testament which God hath enjoined unto you.

²¹ Moreover he sprinkled with blood both the tabernacle, and all the vessels of the ministry.

²² And almost all things are by the law purged with blood; and without shedding of blood is no remission.

²³ It was therefore necessary that the patterns of things in the heavens should be purified with these; but the heavenly things themselves with better sacrifices than these.

²⁴ For Christ is not entered into the holy places made with hands, which are the figures of the true; but into heaven itself, now to appear in the presence of God for us:

²⁵ Nor yet that he should offer himself often, as the high priest entereth into the holy place every year with blood of others;

²⁶ For then must he often have suffered since the foundation of the world: but now once in the end of the world hath he appeared to put away sin by the sacrifice of himself.

²⁷ And as it is appointed unto men once to die, but after this the judgment:

²⁸ So Christ was once offered to bear the sins of many; and unto them that look for him shall he appear the second time without sin unto salvation.

1 Peter 2:9 (KJV)

⁹ But ye are a chosen generation, a royal priesthood, an holy nation, a peculiar people; that ye should shew forth the praises of him who hath called you out of darkness into his marvellous light;

Psalm 100:4

[4] *Enter into his gates with thanksgiving, and into his courts with praise: be thankful unto him, and bless his name.*

Ephesians 5:17-21 (KJV)

[17] *Wherefore be ye not unwise, but understanding what the will of the Lord is.*

[18] *And be not drunk with wine, wherein is excess; but be filled with the Spirit;*

[19] *Speaking to yourselves in psalms and hymns and spiritual songs, singing and making melody in your heart to the Lord;*

[20] *Giving thanks always for all things unto God and the Father in the name of our Lord Jesus Christ;*

[21] *Submitting yourselves one to another in the fear of God.*

Proverbs 6:30-31 (NIV)

[30] *People do not despise a thief if he steals to satisfy his hunger when he is starving.*

[31] *Yet if he is caught, he must pay sevenfold, though it costs him all the wealth of his house.*

Exodus 27:1-8 NIV

The Altar of Burnt Offering

[1] *Build an altar of acacia wood, three cubits high; it is to be square, five cubits long and five cubits wide*

[2] *Make a horn at each of the four corners, so that the horns and the altar are of one piece, and overlay the altar with bronze.*

³ Make all its utensils of bronze—its pots to remove the ashes, and its shovels, sprinkling bowls, meat forks and fire pans.

⁴ Make a grating for it, a bronze network, and make a bronze ring at each of the four corners of the network.

⁵ Put it under the ledge of the altar so that it is halfway up the altar.

⁶ Make poles of acacia wood for the altar and overlay them with bronze.

⁷ The poles are to be inserted into the rings so they will be on two sides of the altar when it is carried.

⁸ Make the altar hollow, out of boards. It is to be made just as you were shown on the mountain.

Psalms 107:2 NKJV

² Let the redeemed of the LORD say so, Whom He has redeemed from the hand of the enemy

Ephesians 1:7 (KJV)

⁷ In whom we have redemption through his blood, the forgiveness of sins, according to the riches of his grace;

Revelation 5:9 (KJV)

⁹ And they sung a new song, saying, Thou art worthy to take the book, and to open the seals thereof: for thou wast slain, and hast redeemed us to God by thy blood out of every kindred, and tongue, and people, and nation;

Romans 3:25 (KJV)

²⁵ Whom God hath set forth to be a propitiation through faith in his blood, to declare his righteousness for the remission of sins that are past, through the forbearance of God;

I John 2:2 (KJV)

² And he is the propitiation for our sins: and not for ours only, but also for the sins of the whole world.

1 John 4:10 (KJV)

¹⁰ Herein is love, not that we loved God, but that he loved us, and sent his Son to be the propitiation for our sins.

Psalms 149

¹ Praise ye the LORD. Sing unto the LORD a new song, and his praise in the congregation of saints.

² Let Israel rejoice in him that made him: let the children of Zion be joyful in their King.

³ Let them praise his name in the dance: let them sing praises unto him with the timbrel and harp.

⁴ For the LORD taketh pleasure in his people: he will beautify the meek with salvation.

⁵ Let the saints be joyful in glory: let them sing aloud upon their beds.

⁶ Let the high praises of God be in their mouth, and a two-edged sword in their hand;

⁷ To execute vengeance upon the heathen, and punishments upon the people;

⁸ To bind their kings with chains, and their nobles with fetters of iron;

⁹ To execute upon them the judgment written: this honour have all his saints. Praise ye the LORD.

Hebrews 12:2 King James Version (KJV)

² Looking unto Jesus the author and finisher of our faith; who for the joy that was set before him endured the cross, despising the shame, and is set down at the right hand of the throne of God.

Titus 3:5

⁵ Not by works of righteousness which we have done but according to his mercy he saved us by the washing of regeneration, and renewing of the Holy Ghost.

Photographs of Interest

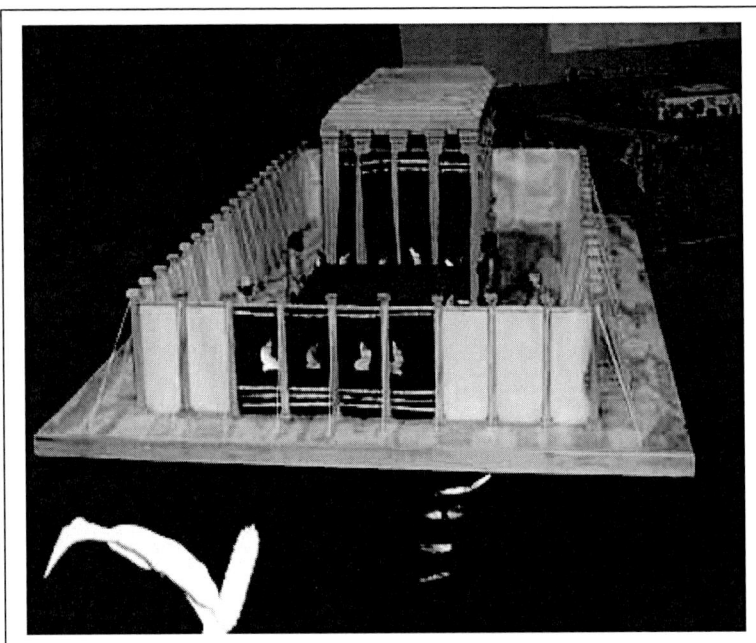

The Tabernacle (view from above)

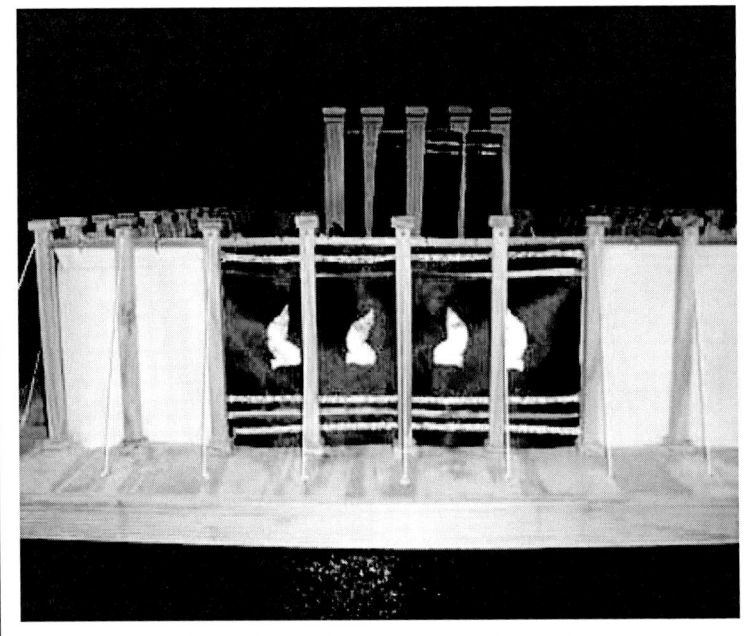

The Gate Entrance (front view)

The Court (right side view of the Tabernacle)

The Brazen Laver

The Ark of the Covenant

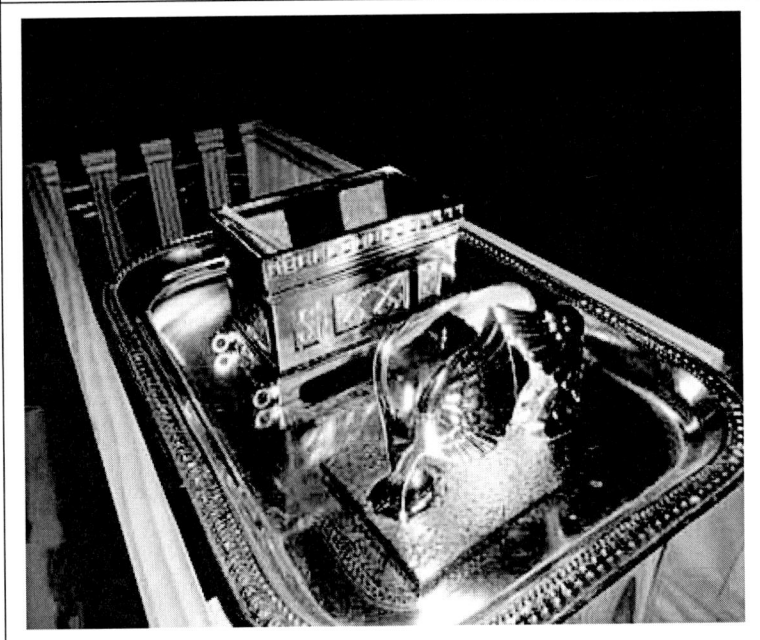

The Ark and the Mercy Seat

Mercy Seat and Lid of the Ark

The Altar of Incense

Candlestand/Golden Lampstand

Candlestand/Golden Lampstand

The Altar of Incense

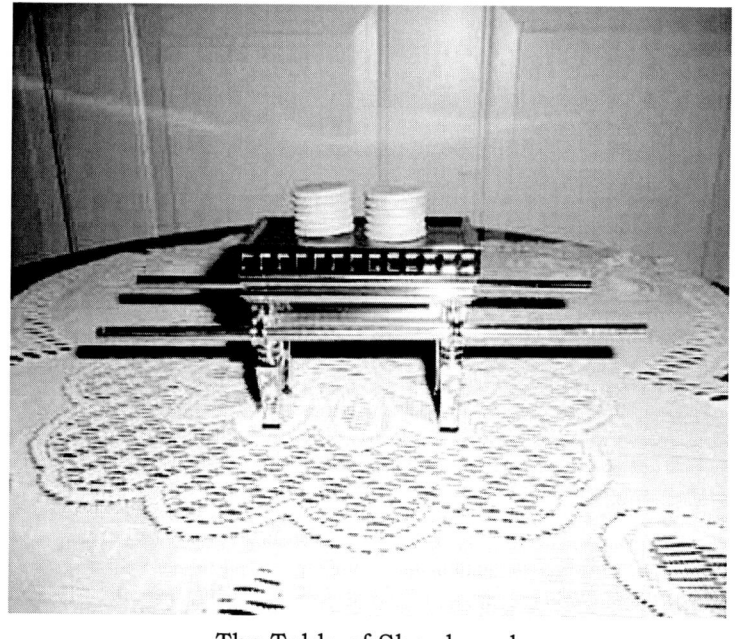

The Table of Shewbread

The Table of Shewbread

Right to Left: Golden Lampstand,
Altar of Incense, Table of Shewbread

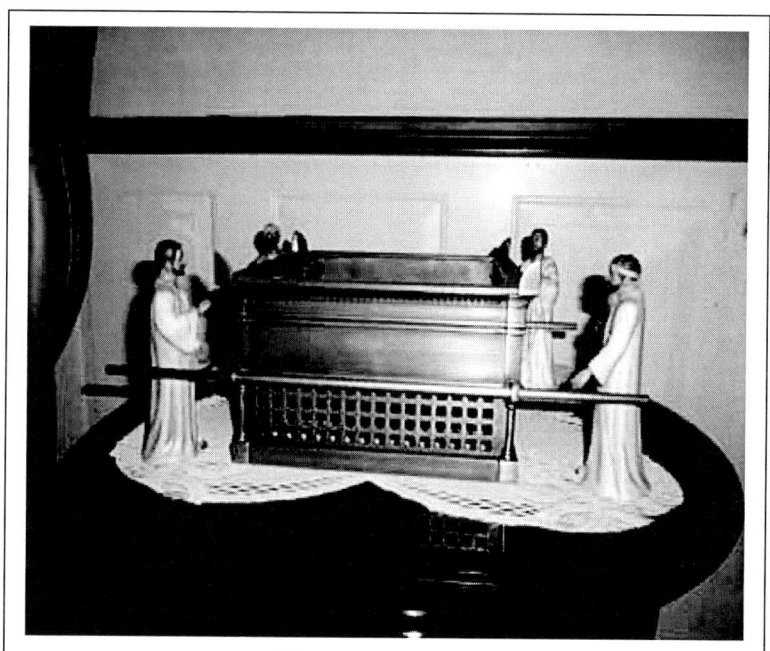

The Brazen Altar

The Brazen Altar Show

Golden Urn (containing the manna, Aaron's Rod and the Stone tablets of the Covenant)

References

Strong, J. -S.T.D., LL.D, -- Comprehensive Concordance of the Bible Dictionaries of the Hebrew and Greek Words of the original with references to the English words.

Unger, M.F.-Bible Dictionary, Revised and updated Edition 1988; the Moody Bible Institute of Chicago

McAllister, J. Dr.; Praise and Worship Video

Holman Illustrated Bible Dictionary, 1999, 2000, 2002, 2004; Holman Bible Publishers, Nashville, Tennessee

Versions of the Bible: KJV; NET; MSG; BBE; NIV

About The Author

Pastor Eleanor is a native of San Antonio, Texas, but currently resides in Amarillo, Texas. She accepted Jesus Christ as Lord and Savior at the age of five and immediately answered the call to music ministry. At an early age she began to lead and harmonize Christian Songs under the guidance of her mother, Vernie Mae Daniels Biser, who was a Music Instructor and Gospel Artist. Pastor Eleanor is married to Richard Murray, who is Bishop of New Light Ministries of Amarillo. She is also the mother of two lovely and talented daughters, Teresa and Kimberly.

Eleanor was ordained as Pastor of the New Light Ministries in 1985. She received her Missionary and Evangelist Licenses in 1990 and was ordained to Pastor the New Light Ministries in 1992. Pastor Eleanor was ordained by Bishop T.D. Jakes of Dallas, Texas and is an active member of the Potter's House International Pastors Association. She is currently a board member of the Gospel Music Workshop of American and an active member of the Texas Mass Choir. Pastor Eleanor also serves as a songwriter, praise and worship leader, musician and choir director. Along with her other services for the kingdom of God, she is the coordinator and administrator for the education department at the New Light Ministries of Amarillo, Texas.

Eleanor holds a Bachelor of Science degree in Business Education from Prairie View A&M University. She acquired additional certifications in C.V.A.E./Office Education from North Texas State University. Graduating with honors (*Cum Laude*), she received her Master's Degree of Theological Biblical Studies from Logos Christian College. Since retirement from public teaching, Eleanor has dedicated her time and services to the New Light Ministries full time.

Healing, restoration, comfort and exhortation are ministered to the Body of Christ through her anointed teaching and demonstration of Praise and Worship. With her dynamic methods and practical teaching, she ushers many into the Presence of God. Eleanor believes the time has come to release her gifts and be a lighthouse in a dark and stormy world, shining forth to the lost, hurt, wounded and sick. Through her gift to teach the word of God and talent of singing, she will be able to guide those in need, to a place of shelter and refuge; offering peace to those who are being tossed to and fro. As she continues to seek God's face, hear His voice and abide under His covering; He will sing and minister through His vessel and be lifted up so all will be drawn unto Him.